THE WOMEN

THE WOMEN

By the Editors of

TIME-LIFE BOOKS

with text by

Joan Swallow Reiter

TIME-LIFE BOOKS / ALEXANDRIA, VIRGINIA

Time-Life Books Inc.
is a wholly owned subsidiary of
TIME INCORPORATED

Founder: Henry R. Luce 1898-1967

Editor-in-Chief: Henry Anatole Grunwald
Chairman of the Board: Andrew Heiskell
President: James R. Shepley
Editorial Director: Ralph Graves
Vice Chairman: Arthur Temple

TIME-LIFE BOOKS INC.

Managing Editor: Jerry Korn
Executive Editor: David Maness
Assistant Managing Editors: Dale M. Brown
(planning), George Constable, Martin Mann,
John Paul Porter
Art Director: Tom Suzuki
Chief of Research: David L. Harrison
Director of Photography: Robert G. Mason
Senior Text Editor: Diana Hirsh
Assistant Art Director: Arnold C. Holeywell
Assistant Chief of Research: Carolyn L. Sackett
Assistant Director of Photography: Dolores A. Littles

Chairman: Joan D. Manley
President: John D. McSweeney
Executive Vice Presidents: Carl G. Jaeger,
John Steven Maxwell, David J. Walsh
Vice Presidents: Peter G. Barnes,
Nicholas Benton (public relations), John L. Canova
(sales), Nicholas J. C. Ingleton (Asia),
James L. Mercer (Europe/South Pacific),
Herbert Sorkin (production), Paul R. Stewart
(promotion)
Personnel Director: Beatrice T. Dobie
Consumer Affairs Director: Carol Flaumenhaft

THE OLD WEST

EDITORIAL STAFF FOR "THE WOMEN"
Editors: Thomas Flaherty, Jim Hicks
Deputy Editor: Gerald Simons
Picture Editor: Donna M. Lucey
Text Editors: Bobbie Conlan-Moore, Lee Hassig,
David Johnson
Designer: Edward Frank
Staff Writers: Russell Adams, Susan Feller,
Margaret Fogarty, Mark Steele
Chief Researchers: Lois Gilman,
Carol Forsyth Mickey
Researchers: Kristin Baker, Karen M. Bates,
Mary G. Burns, Mindy A. Daniels,
Barbara Fleming, Pat Good
Art Assistant: Van W. Carney
Editorial Assistant: Barbara Brownell

EDITORIAL PRODUCTION
Production Editor: Douglas B. Graham
Operations Manager: Gennaro C. Esposito,
Gordon E. Buck (assistant)
Assistant Production Editor: Feliciano Madrid
Quality Control: Robert L. Young (director),
James J. Cox (assistant), Michael G. Wight
(associate)
Art Coordinator: Anne B. Landry
Copy Staff: Susan B. Galloway (chief),
Patricia Graber, Peter Kaufman, Celia Beattie
Picture Department: Linda Hensel
Traffic: Jeanne Potter

THE AUTHOR: Joan Swallow Reiter grew up on a historic pathway to the West. Route 40, referred to since pioneer times as the National Road, wound past her home in Richmond, Indiana, one of the towns that boasted a "Madonna of the Trail" statue memorializing pioneer women of the West. Her own great-great-great-grandparents settled in Indiana Territory in 1807, when it was still forest wilderness. Mrs. Reiter was a writer-editor for TIME-LIFE BOOKS before becoming a freelance based in New York.

THE COVER: Women move west on horseback and by wagon in a romanticized early 1850s painting, *The Pioneers,* by William Ranney. Prairie crossings were long and arduous, and to keep the loads light women could take only the barest necessities for pioneer housekeeping. The frontispiece: Dressed up for the photographer in her Sunday best, a new arrival in a Colorado mining camp puts on a brave display of feminine gentility, undaunted by the frontier surroundings or a scene-stealing burro.

CORRESPONDENTS: Elisabeth Kraemer (Bonn); Margot Hapgood, Dorothy Bacon, Lesley Coleman (London); Susan Jonas, Lucy T. Voulgaris (New York); Maria Vincenza Aloisi, Josephine du Brusle (Paris); Ann Natanson (Rome). Valuable assistance was also provided by: Carolyn T. Chubet, Miriam Hsia (New York).

The editors are indebted to Valerie Moolman, text editor, and Leon Jaroff, writer, for their help with this book.

Library of Congress Cataloging in Publication Data
Time-Life Books.
  The women.
  (The Old West; v. 23)
  Bibliography: p.
  Includes index.
  1. Women—The West. 2. Frontier and pioneer life—The West. I. Reiter, Joan Swallow, 1925-
II. Title. III. Series: The Old West (New York); v. 23.
HQ1418.T55   301.41'2'0978   78-1346
ISBN 0-8094-1514-3
ISBN 0-8094-1513-5 lib. bdg.

CONTENTS

Standing with her youngster in an immense field of wheat, a Wyoming woman epitomizes the self-reliance fostered by Western isolation.

1 | Promise in a lonely land

The West was full of promise for women. To succeed they had to fight off Indian raids and endure starvation, privation and the aching sense of being alone in an endless, empty land. But as partners to their menfolk they performed labor worth more than all of the West's gold by pressing for schools and churches, law and order. Their reward was a sense of competence: "I felt a secret joy," an Oregon woman declared, "in being able to have a power that sets things going."

Some women were not satisfied just to be "the Missus"; they sought fulfillment of long-suppressed aspirations. Thousands homesteaded their own land. Thousands more kept stretching the bounds of a woman's world, vying for jobs normally filled by men and even entering the professions. They demanded the vote and, while the East stood aghast, they had, by 1900, won that right in four Western states.

Three generations of a homesteading family overflow their Oklahoma dugout home in 1901. For women, such large broods were a trial to raise; but the children soon helped with chores and provided companionship in the wilderness.

A stalwart old woman, wearing her best bonnet to dignify her arrival in Oregon, leads her motley team into Baker City, a heavily male mining town. The variety of draft animals suggests that several of her oxen died on the trail.

Two Montana matrons wearing 1870s fashions meet in Helena, a wild mining camp until their likes arrived. When women appeared, said one man, streets grew "passable, clean and quiet" and "pistols were less frequently fired."

Exulting in the freedom of the West, two young women gallop headlong across an open stretch of Oregon grazing land. They also took the liberty of riding astride in divided skirts—a practice considered shocking in the East.

The long, hard trail to new opportunity

One July afternoon in 1905 a festive throng assembled on the grounds of the Lewis and Clark Exposition in Portland, Oregon. Men, women and children from the North, South, East and West had come together to perform a ritual, and they could hardly have chosen a more appropriate spot.

All around them stretched a country rich in beauty and meaning. To the southeast rose the noble white cone of Oregon's Mount Hood, to the north the peak of Washington's Mount St. Helens. To the east lay the great gorge cut by the Columbia River in its foaming plunge westward to the Pacific. Just beyond the fairgrounds flowed the Willamette, along whose watershed the trappers and missionaries, the farmers and orchardists and loggers of pioneer Oregon had carved out a new enclave of civilization. Here, where the Willamette met the Columbia, had sprung up the foremost city of Oregon, its streets bustling this summer day with the myriad visitors in town for the exposition.

The multitude crowding the fairgrounds was more than a mere grab bag of tourists. Shoals of suffragettes swirled about the scene, for the National American Woman Suffrage Association was holding its annual convention in Portland that week. The association's president emeritus, the venerable Susan B. Anthony of Rochester, New York, graced the speaker's platform. At her side was the Northwest's own Abigail Scott Duniway—as dedicated a fighter for women's rights as her Eastern friend and, in fact, a good deal scrappier.

On hand to participate in the proceedings were members of the Improved Order of Red Men, a frater-

Agnes Freeman, her stolid portrait in an ornate Civil War frame, went west in 1865. Tireless, she ran her husband's Nebraska ranch, reared seven children, opened a school and practiced medicine.

nal organization composed, oddly enough, of white men. Some genuine Indians were present, too, including a group of youngsters from a local school and an Alaskan Indian, nervously clearing his throat, who would shortly be called upon to sing a patriotic song.

The purpose for which these people had gathered was to dedicate a statue of Sacajawea, the young Shoshoni wife and mother who had accompanied trailblazers Meriwether Lewis and William Clark on their westward journey 100 years earlier. It was a red-letter day for the ladies, observed the *Oregon Journal,* a day on which they could take "swelling pride in the significance of the occasion—the celebration of a woman's historic achievements."

There was little doubt in the minds of the women present that without Sacajawea, Lewis and Clark would probably never have made it across the crest of the Rockies, the single most difficult barrier they faced in their push to the Pacific Northwest. As long as history endured, the Lewis and Clark expedition would stand as one of mankind's—and womankind's—grandest adventures. Beyond the sheer wonder of the journey lay its political import: when the explorers successfully completed their transcontinental trek, the fledgling United States of America could, for the first time, lay solid claim to the future Oregon Territory.

Cheers rang out when the American flag draping the statue was pulled away and Sacajawea stood revealed: a beautiful and resolute young figure in fringed buckskins, her baby on her back, her outstretched arm forever pointing the way. The statue had been sculpted by a woman, Alice Cooper of Chicago; it was a gift, the citation read, "from the women of the United States in memory of Sacajawea and in honor of the pioneer mothers of old Oregon."

Lest the full meaning of the tribute be lost on some, Abigail Scott Duniway, herself one of the doughtiest

collect and deposit in large hoards. This operation she performed by penetrating the earth with a sharp stick about some small collections of drift wood. Her labour soon proved successful and she procured a good quantity of these roots." Throughout the journey Sacajawea continued to gather roots and berries, contributing substantially to the company's food supply.

But the young Indian's alertness and initiative were soon displayed more dramatically. The white pirogue, Lewis and Clark found, was much less stable than they had imagined. On May 14, while the expedition's leaders were both ashore and the pirogue out in midstream, a sudden gust of wind struck the craft obliquely. Charbonneau—who, Lewis wrote, was not only the "worst steersman of the party" but "perhaps the most timid waterman in the world"—was at the helm; in his fright, Charbonneau steered in the wrong direction.

The pirogue upset. Before it was righted, the boat had nearly filled with water and some of its most valu-

able cargo was swept overboard. Finally, Charbonneau brought the boat under control. With every available hand bailing frantically and hauling sail, the craft made its way to shore "scarcely above the water."

Amid the panic, Sacajawea kept her head. When Lewis surveyed the loss two days later, he remarked in his journal: "The Indian woman to whom I ascribe equal fortitude and resolution, with any person onboard at the time of the accident, caught and preserved most of the light articles which were washed overboard." Thanks to Sacajawea, much of the expedition's irreplaceable equipment had been saved.

As the expedition approached the Great Falls of the Missouri, Sacajawea fell gravely ill. Every member of the party suffered intermittently from influenza, dysentery, fevers or abdominal pains, but the illness of the young Indian woman caused special concern. Lewis and Clark were both skilled in trail medicine, and each tried to allay her suffering—as Lewis said, out of "con-

20

cern as well for the poor object herself, then with a young child in her arms, as from the consideration of her being our only dependence for a friendly negociation with the Snake Indians." Plastered with medicinal barks, dosed with laudanum and with mineral water from a sulfur spring, Sacajawea recovered just in time to make the tedious month-long portage around the Great Falls and into the high country of her people.

July was well advanced before the Shoshoni girl began to recognize the landscape. On the 22nd she assured the expedition leaders they were nearing the three forks—the headwaters of the Missouri, which Lewis and Clark named the Jefferson, Madison and Gallatin rivers. Continuing to point out familiar landmarks, Sacajawea told the expedition leaders on July 28 that they had reached the place where her people had been encamped five years before, and she showed them the exact spot where her party had been attacked by the Hidatsas and herself taken prisoner.

Lewis was anxious to make contact with the Shoshonis as quickly as possible. He pressed ahead with a small party toward a pass in the Bitterroot Mountains along the Continental Divide. There, Sacajawea assured him, her people would be crossing to their summer retreat. Clark and the others, including Sacajawea, were to follow with the bulk of the equipment. Thus it was Lewis and his companions who first made contact with Sacajawea's people and their chief, Cameahwait.

The Shoshonis were not unfriendly. But since the two groups could communicate only by sign language, the Indians grew puzzled and wary when Lewis struggled to describe the separate, larger party of men behind him. Somehow Lewis persuaded Cameahwait and a company of lesser chiefs, warriors and' women to go back with him to meet the main body of the expedition.

The reunion took place on a sparkling day in August when Clark was walking close to the shore of the Beaverhead River with Charbonneau and Sacajawea. Suddenly, according to the official account of the expedition, "Clark saw Sacajawea, who was with her husband 100 yards ahead, begin to dance and show every mark of the most extravagant joy, turning round him and pointing to several Indians, whom he now saw advancing on horseback, sucking her fingers at the same time to indicate that they were of her native tribe." As the Clark group drew nearer to the party of Indians

accompanying Captain Lewis, "a woman made her way through the croud towards Sacajawea, and recognising each other, they embraced with the most tender affection." It turned out that the two young women had been captured in the Hidatsa raid, and "had shared and softened the rigours of their captivity" until one had escaped, "with scarce a hope of ever seeing her friend relieved from the hands of her enemies."

With the ice thus broken, the expedition leaders settled into a powwow with Cameahwait under a shelter of willow brush. Sacajawea was called in to translate the discussion. As the journal described the scene: "She came into the tent, sat down, and was beginning to interpret, when, in the person of Cameahwait, she recognized her brother. She instantly jumped up, and ran and embraced him, throwing over him her blanket, and weeping profusely. The chief himself was moved, though not in the same degree."

He was moved enough, however, to befriend the white men, accept their gifts and supply them with horses to take them across the Rockies.

Elated as she was at seeing her own people after years of separation, Sacajawea chose to journey on with Charbonneau and the expedition. Her mere presence on the grinding haul across the mountains and the subsequent passage down thc Clearwater, Snake and Columbia rivers was of inestimable value. Daily the pathfinders encountered potentially hostile bands of Nez Percé, Flathead or other Indians, all of whom accepted the strangers amicably when they caught sight of Sacajawea and her baby. Her presence, wrote Clark, "reconsiles all the Indians as to our friendly intentions. A woman with a party of men is a token of peace."

When at last they reached the coast on November 8, 1805, the Corps of Discovery was a tattered, bone-weary but jubilant crew. After a journey of more than 4,000 miles, they had reached the Pacific, having carved an indelible path across the wilderness to link the civilized East with the untamed West.

Sacajawea and Charbonneau wintered with the explorers in their camp, Fort Clatsop, near the mouth of the Columbia River, and headed back east with them in spring. Clark had become fond of the Indian woman and her child; he sometimes called Sacajawea "Janey," and he referred frequently to the little boy as "my boy Pomp." How Sacajawea felt about William Clark—

Frontier heroines who never were

Dime novels, launched in the 1860s, invented heroines every bit as intrepid—and unbelievable—as their male counterparts. Embroidering on the real dangers of the West, the authors pitted fictional young women, usually single-handed, against Indian hordes, outlaw bands and slavering carnivores.

No sunbonnets or shapeless calico swathed these protagonists. Hurricane Nell (*right*) wore a "close-fitting suit of buckskin, tastefully fringed and ornamented with Indian beads." Mountain Kate, fresh from confronting a grizzly bear (*opposite*), was royally turned out "in a fancifully-ornamented suit of whitely-bleached doeskin."

In the tradition of Pocahontas, some of the heroines were brave Indian maidens. *Malaeska, The Indian Wife of the White Hunter,* sold briskly. But most heroines were white. In the blood-and-thunder tale of *Bess, The Trapper,* the author stipulated that even though Bess's long black hair might be taken for that of an Indian, her "clear white skin was unmistakably that of a caucasian." And Mountain Kate's "complexion was dark, yet of that rare clearness and purity through which the rapid flow of blood was distinctly visible, showing that no aboriginal taint was in her veins."

Nell and Bess and Kate were permitted to be violent in defense of themselves and their loved ones. But no matter how desperate the circumstances became, they always remained ladies. Their reward was a happy ending, which the novelist usually accomplished by marrying the doughty lasses into polite society. Thus Kate of the pure complexion left the mountains to marry Frank and was welcomed by the elite of St. Louis. And Hurricane Nell gave up garroting outlaws to marry a lawyer from Philadelphia named Cecil.

Imperiled maidens, adventuring in a fictionized West, rode, roped and shot their way through 1870s romances: *Hurricane Nell* Edward L. Wheeler; *Bess, the Trapper* by Lieutenant J. H. Randolph; and *Mountain Kate* by Joseph Badger Jr.

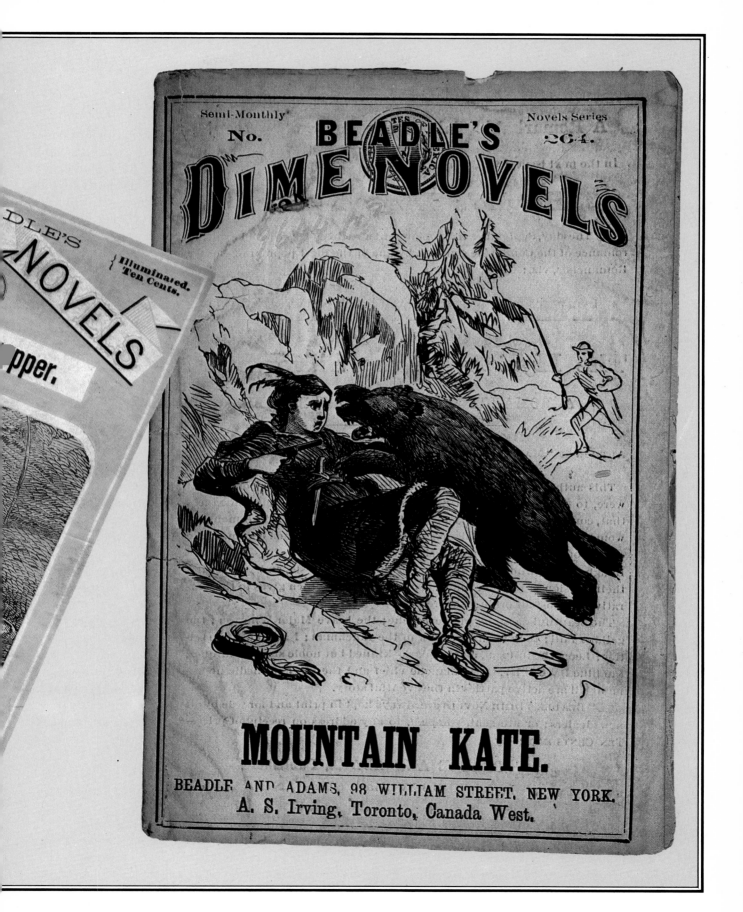

Semi-Monthly

Novels Series

No.

BEADLE'S

264.

DIME NOVELS

Illuminated.
Ten Cents.

MOUNTAIN KATE.

BEADLE AND ADAMS, 98 WILLIAM STREET, NEW YORK.
A. S. Irving, Toronto, Canada West.

who was from all accounts a warmer and more outgoing man than Lewis — was apparent from the little gifts she gave him during the trip: in November a scrap of bread she had been hoarding for her baby, and on Christmas Day two dozen white weasels' tails.

When the Lewis and Clark expedition reached the Mandan villages in August 1806, sixteen months after setting out, Clark paid off Charbonneau — "for his services as an enterpreter the price of a horse and Lodge purchased of him for public Service in all amounting to 500$ 33 1/3 cents" — and bade farewell to the little family. As for Charbonneau's "femme Janey," Clark could never adequately compensate her. "Your woman," he later wrote to Charbonneau, "who accompanied you that long and dangerous and fatiguing route to the Pacific Ocian and back, deserved a greater reward for her attention and service than we had in our power to give her at the Mandans."

What he did was offer to raise and educate the little boy, Pomp, "a butifull promising child," and he repeated the offer until, some five years later, it was accepted. Sacajawea and Charbonneau brought the youngster to Clark in St. Louis; they stayed for a time and then, weary of civilized life, returned to the wilder reaches of the Missourri. Pomp went to school in St. Louis and later in Europe, but in 1829 he returned to the frontier where he was said to be "the best man on foot on the plains or in the Rocky Mountains."

Shoshoni tradition says Sacajawea had a long life of wanderings, an honored old age on the Shoshoni reservation at Wind River, Wyoming, and death at the age of almost 100. But the mists of legend are pierced by two laconic sentences in a fur trader's journal. On December 20, 1812, the clerk at Fort Manuel, a trading post on the upper Missouri, included a terse obituary in his daily log: "This evening the wife of Charbonneau, a Snake squaw, died of a putrid fever. She was the best woman in the fort, aged about 25 years." And thus Sacajawea's unique life journey ended. She had welcomed the white man into the vast, uncharted West and, in a symbolic sense, had blazed a trail for his women to follow.

Into the mountainous landscape pioneered by the Lewis and Clark expedition spilled a swashbuckling assortment of fur trappers and traders. In their search for beaver pelts, big money and the means of transporting their furs and supplies, they discovered a path across the Rockies, through which they eventually drove pack trains and wagons. To the hundreds of thousands of emigrants who would travel the Oregon Trail and its offshoots in the decades to come, the new gateway to the West became known as South Pass — and the wagon train became a symbol of the great overland migration of men, women and children.

In fact, the first white women to cross the Rockies traveled most of the way on horseback, sidesaddle; the wagon in which they were supposed to be riding had a distressing habit of tipping over and breaking down. The year was 1836; the women were Narcissa Whitman and Eliza Spalding, missionaries journeying with their husbands to establish a mission post at Fort Walla Walla, in what later became the state of Washington. When Narcissa arrived at her destination, weary but in good spirits, she described the trip as "an unheard of journey for females." Upon their arrival the two couples were treated to an enthusiastic reception by the Indians, and the American Board of Commissioners for Foreign Missions, an interdenominational Protestant group, thereupon decided to dispatch a second missionary party across the overland trail to join the Whitmans and the Spaldings.

The chosen messengers of the gospel in this second group came together at Independence, Missouri, on April 15, 1838. All were Easterners, and all were newlyweds. William and Mary Gray had come from the state of New York, where they had been married in February. Cushing and Myra Eells, Elkanah and Mary Walker, Asa and Sarah Smith all hailed from New England; all had been married a month or less. Of the four men, only Gray had been West before and was prepared for such trail activities as loading pack animals and hunting game. The women were well trained in household duties, but they had no inkling of what it would be like to prepare food on the trail in a torrential rainstorm over a fire of prairie coal — their delicate euphemism for buffalo dung.

Nor had any of the newlyweds anticipated how deeply they would yearn for privacy, which was denied them on the trail not only in sleeping arrangements but also in regard to toilet functions, for in desert country or plains there often was not a rock or shrub to screen them. Above all, they would have to learn to get along together. They were sometimes short-tempered and inconsiderate; by temperament the four couples had little in common other than their heartfelt desire to bring Christianity to the Indians, and they did not particularly like each other.

The party spent several days at Independence, making the final preparations for their journey. William Gray supervised the purchase of a light wagon, 25 horses and mules, nine yearling heifers and four milch cows, and, according to Myra Eells, "a hundred and sixty pounds of flour, fifty-seven pounds of rice, twenty or twenty-five pounds of sugar, a little pepper and salt." Prior to the group's departure, the women occupied themselves busily with such traditionally feminine tasks as washing, ironing and sewing—the unusual twist being that now they were sewing shelters and bags to hold their supplies.

By April 21 the party had arrived saddlesore at Westport, Missouri, having traveled 12 miles from Independence to join up for greater safety with the American Fur Company's large caravan of about 60 men, 17 carts and wagons, and some 200 horses and mules. The plan was to travel along with the fur traders to their rendezvous point in the Rockies.

The missionaries left Westport on April 23. Writing to her family on the following evening Mary Walker complained about sharing a small tent, with nothing but a curtain to separate two families: "Mr. and Mrs. Smith are sleeping loudly in the other part of the tent." Mary's letter gave only the slightest hint that the Smiths were not altogether to her liking, and none at all that she was uneasy about her relationship with her husband, Elkanah, whom she usually referred to as "husband," "Mr. Walker" or simply "W." To her diary she confided that she would "feel much better if Mr. W. would only treat me with more cordiality. It is so hard to please him I almost despair of ever being able. If I stir it is forwardness, if I am still, it is inactivity. I keep trying to please but sometimes I feel it is no use. May God help me to walk discretely, do right and please my husband."

The travelers had ridden 23 miles that day and found themselves almost too exhausted to eat. On the next day Mary Walker wrote: "Rode 21 miles without alighting. Had a long bawl. Husband spoke so

cross I could scarcely bare it, but he seemed to pity me a little when he found how bad I felt."

The fur company's caravan traveled, Myra Eells wrote, in a lumbering procession about half a mile long, and its pace was slow—seldom faster than a fast walk. "When we are fairly on our way we have much the appearance of a large funeral procession in the States." The crew was kindly, if somewhat rowdy, and included the Indian wives and children of some of the traders. Every man and woman was expected to know and do his own work, the missionaries included. Each of the men in the mission party had charge of several animals, to pack, harness, drive, picket and feed. The women cooked, baked bread and pies, and washed clothes whenever they could. Considering their lack of experience, they adapted to trail life remarkably quickly.

On May 3, camping near a creek after riding 14 miles, Myra Eells, Mary Gray and Mary Walker decided it was a good time to do a wash. While they gathered wood for a fire, Sarah Smith prepared dinner and did some baking. "We dressed in our night dresses for washing," Myra wrote, "built a fire almost in the center of the creek on some stones, warmed some water, commenced washing in the kettles because we had nothing else to supply the place of wash-tubs." With the ingenuity born of necessity, they discovered that "we could heat water, wash, boil and rince our clothes in the same kettle."

Yet, in spite of the mission group's apparent adaptability, the small rifts in the fabric of their personal relationships were beginning to widen. Mary Walker noted in her journal: "Mr. Smith undertook to help Mr. W. correct me for dictating to Mr. Gray. I think the reproof quite unmerited." And later, a twinge of jealousy: "Feel so tried with Mr. W. I know not what to do. He seems to think more of Mrs. Smith than of me. Spends a great deal more time in her society than in mine. I feel that I am cruelly neglected.

"We have a strange company of Missionaries," Mary Walker concluded. "Scarcely one who is not intolerable on some account."

Far more often than the women complained in their journals, they simply stated the hard facts:

Myra Eells, May 13: "Arise this morning, put on our clothes wet as when we took off, and prepare for a long ride. Moved camp at 7; ride 8 hours, 25 miles—

A westering woman, pausing for a meal with her husband in a Kansas meadow, clings to a symbol of their past: a clean white tablecloth.

without food for ourselves or animals. I do not get off my horse during the whole distance."

Mary Walker, May 17: "In the night it stormed tremendously. Our tent scarcely screened us at all. Our bed was utterly flooded."

Sarah Smith, May 19: "Traveled 25 miles up the Platte river. We have been troubled with gnats along this river. The bite is much worse than the musquito & we are all handsomely bitten."

Mary Walker, May 22: "No wood. Water freezes in the basin."

Myra Eells, May 25: "Mr. Eells and myself hardly able to sit up, but obliged to eat, drink and work as though we were well. Think it is trying."

Trying indeed. By this time a daily diet of buffalo tongues and humps was having an undesirable effect on Eastern stomachs, adding greatly to the everyday strains of travel. Yet perhaps the deepest cause of distress to the four couples continued to be the lack of privacy. Sarah Smith wrote wistfully: "One thing I greatly desire of which I must be deprived, that is retirement. The tent with the two families is the only place for prayers. If we seek the prairie it is an open plain, without a shade or rock or even a hill to hide us from the gaze of a noisy company. At noon the umbrella is our only shelter. When possible Mr. Smith & myself have gone to some ravine or tree & there prayed, but even there have often been disturbed."

Though the women sometimes resented each other, they shared an understanding of women's feelings, and there were times when they could offer a mutual comfort that the men could not. Once when the drenched company was camped on the banks of the North Platte, waiting for heavy rains to let up so they could cross, Mary Walker—a sturdy farmer's daughter and generally the most spirited of the group—suddenly dissolved into tears. "I asked her why she cried," said Sarah Smith, herself muddy and cold. "She said to think how comfortable her father's hogs were. This made us both laugh and cry together."

Before the day was over, the skies had cleared and the caravan crossed the Platte. The missionaries traveled on with lighter hearts, buoyed by the sight of snow-capped peaks on the far horizon. On June 21, 1838, the caravan arrived at the rendezvous site to await guides for the next stage of their journey—and,

Plain styles for a rigorous life

Women preparing for the journey west were advised to take no fine clothing, only "things suitable for everyday wear," such as "a calico frock, plainly made, no hoops, and sun-bonnet." Most homesteading brides could not resist bringing their trousseau gowns of velvet and silk, copied from the Paris-inspired designs in *Godey's Lady's Book (opposite)*. But even if such finery survived the journey, it met with a sad fate. One woman's best dresses all had trains and, she said ruefully, "I trailed them around over my dirt floors until I wore them out."

As Westerners, women quickly learned frontier practicality, stitching up plain and durable dresses. Those who were clever with a needle lengthened the life of their worn-out finery by reusing salvageable cloth in simplified versions of *Godey's* latest styles.

Some women invented garments to suit their new Western chores. A few, annoyed by long skirts that forced them to ride sidesaddle while they tended cattle, dared to create outfits that permitted them to ride comfortably astride: shorter skirts with blue-denim knickers to wear underneath.

The hoopless, straight skirt of this cotton dress would have made it out of fashion back East. But with its bodice lined with canvas for extra strength and warmth, it was ideal for the pioneer woman who reportedly wore it all the way to Oregon.

A hand-sewn cape decorated with blue roses was worn by Elizabeth Stewart en route to the West in 1852. Before reaching her destination, she died in a wagontrain epidemic and was buried by the trail.

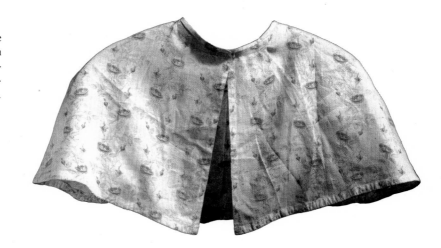

A slat bonnet, so called because it was stiffened by removable wooden splints, was an essential item for homesteading women intent on protecting their fair complexions from the merciless Western sun.

An 1848 issue of *Godey's Lady's Book* showed its readers the billowing Paris gowns then in vogue in the East. Western readers adapting the design might have had to substitute cotton for the prescribed silk.

while waiting, to participate in the great annual trading convention and sporting event staged by the mountain men and their Indian friends.

Most years the rendezvous was held along the Green River, west of the Continental Divide. This summer, however, it convened at the junction of the Pope Agie—often spelled Popeasia—and the Wind rivers, on the eastern side of the Divide. So that none of the usual revelers would miss the fun, somebody—Mary Walker thought it was the famous mountain man, Jim Bridger—had posted a sign on the door of an old storehouse at the Green River site: "Come to Popeasia; plenty of whiskey and white women."

The invitation was swiftly acted upon. Trader Joe Walker showed up in a couple of days with a large company of men. Jim Bridger himself whooped into Popeasia some 10 days later, with "about 100 men & perhaps 60 Indian females & a great number of half breed children," whose arrival was "attended with firing of guns & noisy shouts."

If the men were disappointed that the white women were missionaries, they hid their feelings gallantly and did their good-humored best to make the ladies welcome. A band of Bridger's men came to the missionaries' tents to serenade them "with firing, drumming, singing and dancing." When not thus entertaining, the men gambled, quarreled, told each other uproarious tales and drank prodigiously; their Indian wives and children sang and did scalp dances for the visitors.

Though they were surrounded by hundreds of cursing, carousing roughnecks, the decorous young missionary women from the East treated their small corner of the mountain wilderness as if it were their own backyard. They gathered wild currants and gooseberries, did their laundry, cooked, repaired their own clothes and cut dresses for the trappers' wives out of calico brought to the rendezvous by the traders.

Yet they were anxious to move on, and it was with relief and rejoicing that they welcomed to the rendezvous a party led by a Hudson's Bay Company man who had arranged with William Gray to take them as far west as Fort Hall on the Snake River. On July 12, the missionaries left the rendezvous behind them and followed their new guides to Fort Hall, where they were met by a friendly band of Nez Percé Indians sent from the Oregon mission to take them the rest of the

way to Fort Walla Walla. By the end of August, their toilsome journey was over.

"I can hardly describe my feelings on reaching here," wrote Sarah Smith. "The place so long desired to see. I could hardly believe that the long journey was accomplished & I had found a home."

A home in the West. It was an appealing idea. The news of the missionary women's successful crossing of the Rockies spawned great excitement in the Northern and Eastern states. "This shows, we think," suggested the editor of a Massachusetts magazine, "the feasibility of this route for ladies, and even children." A spark was ignited: what missionary women could do, so could other women—family women, even single women, with no particular skills and no other cause than to pull up stakes and build a new life in the West; women who realized that the scarcity of their sex in the frontierland presented marvelous opportunities; women yearning to shake off the shackles of conventional society and simply be themselves.

Between 1840 and 1869 (when the transcontinental railroad was completed), some 350,000 people flowed through the South Pass gateway to the far reaches of the West. Tens of thousands of them were women. Late each spring the emigrants gathered at prearranged spots along the Missouri and moved out in caravans of anywhere from a few wagons to several hundred. For six months they would drag along at 15 to 20 miles a day, a pace dictated by slow-moving oxen hauling heavy loads, until the survivors reached an unfamiliar destination some 2,000 miles away.

It was especially hard for the women to turn their backs on parents, other relatives and old friends, knowing that they would almost certainly never see them again. It was hard, too, to leave behind cherished furnishings and small, comforting treasures. Space in the wagons and on the pack animals was at such a premium that it was all the men could do to find room for tents, weapons, tools, basic clothing, cooking utensils, medicines and staple foods, never mind the special articles that made a home a home or a woman feel like a woman. Knowing that they must take only the most necessary items, women went to great lengths to tuck in things *they* considered essential: seeds from flowers and shrubs that grew in their gardens at home, little trinkets and wrappings for Christmas, a well-loved book, a few daguerreotypes, a mirror.

With or without the small luxuries, women brought a sense of home and stability to the villages on wheels that were the wagon trains. Catherine Margaret Haun, who made the overland journey from Iowa to California with her husband in 1849, listed the ways in which women "exerted a good influence" on her wagon train: "The men did not take such risks with Indians and thereby avoided conflict; were more alert about the care of the teams and seldom had accidents; more attention was paid to cleanliness and sanitation and, lastly but not of less importance, the meals were more regular and better cooked thus preventing much sickness and there was less waste of food." In fact, a woman's role on the trail was not a great deal different from her role in the home; it merely involved more work, under the most primitive circumstances, and allowed hardly any time for sociability or rest.

No allowances were made for women's special needs. A one-day stopover was grudgingly permitted for a woman to give birth to a child, but labor pains or weakness after childbirth were considered no excuse for dallying. Nor did the women expect special treatment. On the morning after the birth of her baby, Mrs. Phoebe Judson herself urged the wagon train to move on — but noted with appreciation that Mr. Judson "drove over the stones as carefully as though they were eggs."

Rarely did a wagon train include a doctor, and ague, fever, dysentery, diarrhea and cholera went untreated save by home remedies or by nostrums sold by quacks at Independence and St. Joseph.

Cholera struck frequently and was usually fatal. Mary Jane Long, after crossing with her parents and other relatives in 1852, described an all too common experience: "We reached the Platte River, Cholera broke out, and Uncle Silas' family not being strong after measles, he was the first to take down with it and lived only a short time. We had to make a rough box from planks taken out of the wagons and we wrapped his body in bed clothes and buried him." Within the next few days, two of Uncle Silas' sons were stricken, lived briefly and were buried one after the other. The three lonely graves of one family lay miles apart.

Not all trail deaths came from illness. People drowned at river crossings; toddlers fell from wagons and died when the wheels passed over them. Such tragedies took their toll on the spirit, but equally corrosive was the succession of small misfortunes: minor accidents, sudden fears, seemingly endless discomforts and drudgeries that gnawed at a woman's resolve. Children strayed and were lost for hours. Mules bolted and wagons tipped over. Long-stored, carefully rationed food supplies became tainted and had to be discarded. When the going got rough on steep mountain trails and the wagons had to be lightened, every item not essential to survival — bureaus, chests, chairs and treasured family memorabilia — was discarded, leaving the women stripped of all that meant comfort and home.

There were times when the pioneer spirit was strained to the breaking point. Lavinia Honeyman Porter, who went west in 1860 with her husband, James, and a small son, was at first appalled by the onslaught of the elements and the threat of "wild beasts and other dangers." She grew depressed by the monotony of the journey, the drudgery of camp work and a feeling of utter loneliness. "I would make a brave effort to be cheerful and patient until the camp work was done. Then starting out ahead of the team and my men folks, when I thought I had gone beyond hearing distance, I would throw myself down on the unfriendly desert and give way like a child to sobs and tears, wishing myself back home with my friends and chiding myself for consenting to take this wild goose chase."

Men on the trail, Lavinia Porter found, were far less accommodating than they had been back home. Single-minded in the performance of their daily rituals — getting and keeping the wagon train on the road, stopping only for meals and rest — they were in no mood to lend a hand to their women. One day, weary of searching for buffalo chips for the evening campfire, Lavinia spotted a grove of cottonwood trees about half a mile off the trail and asked her husband to make a slight detour so the party could lay in a stock of firewood. James refused; Lavinia dug in her heels. "I was feeling somewhat under the weather and unusually tired," she wrote, "and crawling into the wagon told them if they wanted fuel for the evening meal they could get it themselves and cook the meal also, and laying my head down on a pillow, I cried myself to sleep."

James finally fixed dinner and took it to Lavinia in the wagon. But despite his belated gesture, relations

Treasured possessions that survived the trek

Susannah Bristow wearing a house-cap.

"What to take and what to leave behind us was the problem." So said a young westbound wife who found her wagon dismayingly uncommodious. "Many of our most cherished treasures had to be left to give place to the more necessary articles." The treasures that did begin the overland journeys—items ranging from oak chests to brittle teacups—were taken not because they were essential but because they were symbols of the family's continuity and the civilization they had left behind.

But, sadly, the first things jettisoned as the wagon trains struggled into the foothills were those precious symbols—the china, books, furniture, knickknacks. Such possessions as did make the entire trip—like Susannah Bristow's Bible *(below)* and flo-blue china *(opposite)*—became museum pieces, valuable mainly because they survived. They brought a touch of comfort and familiarity to a rude cabin in an unfamiliar land.

The flo-blue china was part of the dowry Susannah had brought to her marriage with Elijah Bristow in 1812. She had carried it with her from Tennessee to Kentucky in 1820 and to Illinois a few years later. By the time Elijah went on ahead to Oregon, Susannah had been accumulating possessions for almost 35 years of married life. However, her backlog of pioneer experience helped her plan the logistics of her last, most arduous move. When Elijah sent for her, she sold their farm and everything she could not bring. Susannah then packed her pared-down treasures and journeyed west with her eight children and two grandchildren.

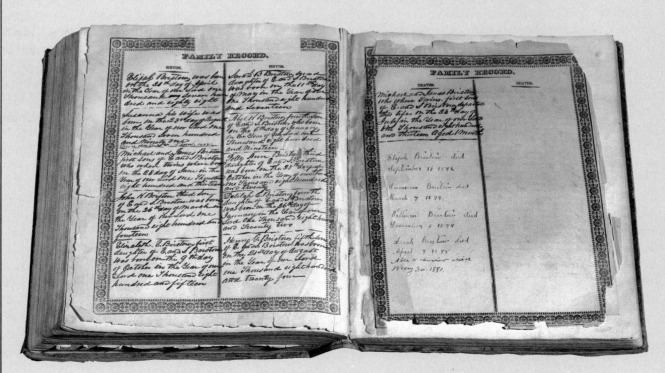

The family record in Susannah's Bible dates from the birth of her husband, Elijah, in 1788.

The blanket-wrapped Bristow china rode safely to Oregon in leather-covered trunks.

Glasses survived the Oregon trek.

The Bristow youngsters may have used this slate for trailside lessons.

between husband and wife remained cool for weeks.

In more than a few instances on the trail, a woman became so distraught that she would flatly refuse to go on. One September day in 1847, Mrs. Elizabeth Geer witnessed a marital showdown precipitated by a woman who had come to the end of her tether.

"This morning," wrote Mrs. Geer, "one company moved on, except one family. The woman got mad and wouldn't budge, nor let the children go. He had his cattle hitched on for three hours and coaxing her to go, but she would not stir." Three other men went to the husband's aid, took the children from the woman and put them in the wagon.

"Her husband drove off and left her sitting. She got up, took the back track and traveled out of sight. Cut across, overtook her husband. Meantime he sent his boy back to camp after a horse that he had left and when she came up her husband says, 'Did you meet John?' 'Yes,' was the reply, 'and I picked up a stone and knocked out his brains.'" The husband went back to ascertain the truth of this hysterical tale, and while he was gone she set one of his wagons on fire. "He saw the flames and came running and put it out, and then mustered up spunk enough to give her a good flogging."

If the incident demonstrates the depths of despair to which a pioneer woman could sink—as well as the subservience of women in a man's world—it also throws into sharp relief the incredible fortitude of other women facing the same, and even more harrowing, circumstances. Sarah Bayliss Royce was one of these.

More than any other year of the great American pilgrimage, 1849 was the year of the man—the adventurous Argonaut who left his wife, family or sweetheart behind to join the quest for California gold. Josiah Royce, however, took his small family with him on what turned out to be one of the loneliest and grimmest journeys a woman ever endured.

Although the favored time of departure from staging points along the Missouri was late April or early May, it was already June when Josiah, his wife, Sarah, and their two-year-old, Mary, left Council Bluffs with a wagon train of strangers. Near the end of August they reached Salt Lake City. Late as it was in the travel season—snow could block the passes through the Sierra Nevada range anytime after mid-October—the

company broke up; each man made his own arrangements to get to the mountains as quickly as possible.

From the Mormons, the Royces received directions to the lower end of the Humboldt River, known as the Sink. Instructions for the rest of the route were confusing and full of discouraging references to poor camping sites and scarce water. However, before reaching the Humboldt, the Royces were told, they would encounter a band of Mormons returning from a summer gold hunt in California. From these seasoned travelers they could learn the best way to cross a stretch of desert to the Carson River and the foot of the Sierras.

On August 30 the young couple and their child left Salt Lake City, accompanied by one old man who was desperately anxious to reach California but had no means of his own to get there. They had a solitary wagon drawn by a three-yoke team of oxen and lightly loaded—in the interest of speed—with provisions intended to last through the deserts and mountains ahead.

They had traveled only a few days across the Great Salt Desert when they were approached by two young men, traveling with only a horse and a mule, who asked to accompany them. The Royce party welcomed them: the more company, the more protection for all. Unfortunately, the new members of the party had very little food; within a few days they were begging for a share of the Royces' meager provisions. The young men hunted every day to supplement the supply of provisions. But game was scarce in the desert, and the hunters contributed little more than an occasional rabbit to the diminishing larder. "Still we kept on, sharing, and hoping for the best," recalled Sarah in the memoirs she wrote 30 years later.

In mid-September the Royces met the band of Mormons they had been told to expect. Tracing out the route in the sand with a stick, the leader carefully explained how they were to get from the Sink of the Humboldt to the Carson River. But there was one detour they had to make, he said, before crossing the barren desert, where there would be no feed for the oxen and no water for man or beast. About two or three miles after the Sink they would see a plain wagon track forking off to the left. They were to follow this track, and within two or three miles from the main road it would bring them to a grassy meadow, where they would find plenty of feed and several wells of clean,

fresh water. Here they must let the oxen rest and feed for a few days while the men cut as much hay as the already crowded wagon could carry and fill every available vessel with water. Thus supplied, the Royce party should be able to reach the Carson River.

The Royces moved on "with renewed cheerfulness and energy." On October 2, they reached the head of Humboldt Lake—"which, at this late period in the dry season, was utterly destitute of water, the river having sunk gradually in the sand, until, hereabout it entirely disappeared." They were now, they thought, about 10 miles from the Sink. In fact, they were already there.

Unaware that the cutoff was only two or three miles away, the Royces and their companions rose at 2 a.m. the next morning, expecting to travel 12 or 13 miles and get to the meadow by noon, which would give them half a day to set up camp and get ready for work.

Under the desert moon, the sand and even the scattered sagebrush took on the same grayish-white look, and at times it was hard to pick out the trail. With dawn the going got easier, and as the sun climbed, the party began to look anxiously for the Sink. It was nearly noon when they came upon some holes and concluded that they had reached the Sink. The company hurried on to find the fork in the road. Hours passed. The sun dipped lower, and as night approached, a grim realization gripped the party: "We had passed the forks of the road before daylight that morning, and were now miles out on the desert without a mouthful of food for the cattle and only two or three quarts of water in a little cask." There was nothing to do but stop for the night and try to work things out in the morning.

Precious hours trickled away the next day while the five adults mulled over their predicament and vainly searched the horizon for another track. The most pressing problem was to keep the oxen alive, and to do this the Royces found a temporary solution: their beds. Josiah and Sarah had a mattress tick into which they had put a little fresh hay before leaving Salt Lake City, and the old man also had a small straw mattress. With this pathetic source of supply, the animals might be kept from collapsing for another few hours. But they could not possibly hold out as far as the Carson River.

Doling out a few mouthfuls to each of the oxen, the forlorn travelers took a small noon meal and stretched out on the sand for a nap. But Sarah could not sleep for

thinking of how short a time their few resources would last and what would happen "unless fresh strength came soon from somewhere." She looked at the sleeping men, and at Mary, sleeping too. "How still it was. Only the sound of a few feeble breaths. It would not take many hours of starvation to quiet them forever."

After waking, Josiah gazed around from the top of a ridge, saw nothing encouraging and decided, with Sarah, to turn back. "Turn back! What a chill the words sent through one. *Turn back,* on a journey like that; in which every mile had been gained by most earnest labor. And now for miles we were to *go back*."

The Royces braced themselves for a journey back of not less than 14 to 16 miles. Next morning, Josiah fed the cattle the last mouthfuls of fodder from the mattresses and Sarah made coffee with nearly the last of the water. Little Mary was now the main concern, for it was well known that a child could not last long without water, and her mother resolved to take scarcely any of the remaining water for herself.

Sarah walked ahead of the wagon and worried about her baby girl. "When my little one, from the wagon behind me, called out, 'Mamma I want a drink'—I stopped, gave her some, noted that there were but a few swallows left, then mechanically pressed onward again, alone, repeating, over and over again, the words, 'Let me not see the death of the child.'"

It was a few hours later, when the oxen were moving with heads so low and feet so slow that it seemed they must collapse at any minute, that shouts of triumph came from the two young men, who rode a few hundred yards ahead. "Grass and water!" they yelled. "Grass and water!" Throwing their hats into the air and waving exuberantly, they led the way to the meadow.

Animals and humans slaked their thirst and rested that afternoon. Next day, the men cut grass and spread it out to dry. Sarah drew water and rearranged the wagon to make as much room as possible for water and hay; then she cooked the last of the party's meat and most of the small remaining stock of dried food.

The Royces' pause was barely long enough to rest the oxen. Then they embarked once more upon the sea of sand, "this time to cross or die." During the second day out two of their oxen gave up and fell prostrate on the ground. The Royces hurried on as quickly as they could with the two surviving yoke, hoping to catch

(4—404.)

THE UNITED STATES OF AMERICA,

To all to whom these presents shall come, Greeting:

Homestead Certificate No. *5071*

APPLICATION *7718*

Whereas There has been deposited in the General Land Office of the United States a Certificate of the Register of the Land Office at *Raleigh Nebraska* whereby it appears that, pursuant to the Act of Congress approved 20th May, 1862, "To secure Homesteads to actual Settlers on the Public Domain," and the acts supplemental thereto, the claim of *Josephine Howard* has been established and duly consummated, in conformity to law, for the *North West quarter of section eleven in township twenty three North of range eleven West of the Sixth Principal Meridian in Nebraska containing one hundred and sixty acres* according to the Official Plat of the survey of the said Land, returned to the General Land Office by the Surveyor General:

Now know ye, That there is, therefore, granted by the United States unto the said *Josephine Howard* the tract of Land above described: TO HAVE AND TO HOLD the said tract of Land, with the appurtenances thereof, unto the said *Josephine Howard* and to *her* heirs and assigns forever.

In testimony whereof, I, *Benjamin Harrison*, President of the United States of America, have caused these letters to be made Patent, and the Seal of the General Land Office to be hereunto affixed.

Given under my hand, at the City of Washington, the *twenty seventh* day of *March*, in the year of our Lord one thousand eight hundred and *eighty nine*, and of the Independence of the United States the one hundred and *thirteenth*.

BY THE PRESIDENT: *Benjamin Harrison*

By *M. McKean*, Secretary.

Obie Ross, Recorder of the General Land Office.

Recorded, Vol. *9*, Page *434*

---

sight of the Carson River before the blazing heat caught up with them next day.

They traveled through the night and as dawn approached, the animals drank the last of the water and at sunup ate the last of their hay. For several miles, as the sun rose higher, not a word was spoken. Then, finally, a low, dark line appeared on the horizon; the oxen raised their heads, bellowed softly, and picked up pace. They had smelled the water of the Carson River.

Early in the afternoon the party rested in the shade of the trees along the riverbank while the oxen fed, drank and cooled themselves in the water. The desert was conquered; now there was only the great obstacle of the Sierra Nevada to face.

Progress toward the foothills was dishearteningly slow, and the Royces' hope of reaching the upland ravines before they were filled with snow began to fade. On October 12, the travelers gazed up a steep incline and wondered how they could possibly ascend it.

Then, in a cloud of dust, two horsemen, each leading a fresh mule, came cantering down a mountain trail toward them. Buckskin sleeves flapping like wings on either side of them, the two looked for all the world like heaven-sent messengers, and Sarah devoutly concluded that was what they were. The men offered a more mundane explanation: they were from the Relief Company "sent out by order of the United States Government to help the late emigrants over the mountains."

Guiding the grateful travelers to a campsite by a spring in the hills, the two men helped repack the party's gear on the animals so they could abandon their wagon—they had to make all possible speed while the spell of clear weather lasted. They gave clear instructions for getting over the mountains by the safest and quickest way and galloped back to Truckee Pass.

A week later the Royces and their companions crossed the summit and began their descent of the western slope of the Sierra Nevada. Exultantly, Sarah looked down—"*down,* far over constantly descending hills, to where a soft haze sent up a warm, rosy glow that seemed to me a smile of welcome"—and knew that she was gazing at the Sacramento Valley.

Long afterward, writing about her journey at the request of her son, Sarah Royce recalled her thoughts at that time, the thoughts of a pioneer woman who had come within reach of a dreamed-of destination: "California, land of sunny skies—that was my first look into your smiling face. I loved you from that moment, for you seemed to welcome me with loving look into rest and safety. However brave a face I might have put on most of the time, I knew my coward heart was yearning all the while for a home-nest and a welcome."

A self-sufficient woman, pioneering in southern California, receives the hard-earned patent to her homestead from a land agent. In some parts of the West, 15 per cent of the homesteaders were lone women, unmarried or widowed.

2 | The great marriage boom

Weddings, like Christmas trees and churchgoing, came West with women. For a bride on the frontier, the familiar wedding ceremony was a reassuring prelude to the unknown life ahead.

Getting married had an equal, if different, appeal for men. In areas where a man's only human companions for months at a time were other men, the march to the altar sometimes resembled a stampede when marriageable females arrived. Ridiculing the frenzied wife-seeking of the early Pacific Northwest, one woman said men proposed to "tearful widows of a fortnight and to little girls busy with mudpies."

Laws that promoted westward expansion sparked a rash of marriages for reasons other than romance. Under the Donation Land Act of 1850 in Oregon Territory a husband and wife were entitled to twice the acreage a single man could claim. A wife also meant extra hands—her own and those of the children who would follow —to make the improvements required by law on a homesteader's claim.

Ironically, the marriage that provided companionship and free labor often cast women into a life, as one rancher's wife said, "lonely in the extreme."

Weddings provided a rare occasion for isolated women to enjoy a formal social event. Buoyed by the festivities, the bride assumed the role that her marriage certificate described as "helpmeet." As a frontier wife, her future would be, more than that of her Eastern sisters, a continual test of the familiar words: "for better or for worse."

Just married to a Wyoming sheepherder, Ohio-born Sedda Hemry learns how to ride. Living in a covered wagon, she saw no other white women for six months.

In the 1890s when this couple married in Spivey, Kansas, Western church weddings were a well-entrenched institution, complete with organist and decorations. The church itself was built with boards salvaged from an old saloon.

On her wedding day in the 1880s, a young bride stands next to her new husband and among his family—the McMillans—at the door of their cabin near Orting, Washington. Before she joined the family, her mother-in-law *(center)* kept house for all nine male McMillans.

Stalwart nurturers of family life

One evening at the height of the California gold rush an audience of grizzled miners sat crowded in a makeshift theater watching a play. Gradually their attention was diverted by a noise that rose above the dialogue onstage. The sound was unmistakable, but incredible. Somewhere *a baby was crying*. A murmur of excitement swept through the house. Craning their necks, the astonished men saw in their midst an embarrassed woman trying to hush the child she held in her arms. One old miner leaped to his feet. "Stop the show," he bellowed at the actors, "so everybody can hear the baby!" Applause rang through the theater, and soon someone was passing a hat to collect an offering. The first baby! In any mining camp that was a milestone ranking just after the first woman.

A turn-of-the-century historian of the West had an explanation for the miners' reaction: "With the coming of women and children came also the graces of life, better social order and conditions, and increased regard for the amenities of existence." The first California census, taken 1850, revealed that women made up less than 10 per cent of the white population. No wonder any mention that this dreary statistic was beginning to change was met with whoops of joy. The San Francisco newspaper *Alta California* of June 27, 1851, reported "a most marked increase of the gentler sex" in recent months. "Both during the day and evening," rejoiced the writer, "the rustling of silks and soft musical voices are quite familiar sounds, and with the silent accompaniment of fresh blooming and pleasant faces, exercises a most pleasurable influence over the minds of the male portion of our citizens."

Marriage certificates—some embellished with photographs—were proudly displayed in homes as symbols of the new stability that women brought to the West.

To be a mate, companion and homemaker to her husband, to bear and raise children—this had been a woman's traditional destiny, and it was the role the vast majority of women played in settling the frontier. Yet the familiar terrain of marriage and motherhood became a novel testing ground for the Western woman, with problems both spiritual and physical that her sisters back East rarely had to face. She was uprooted from family and friends, isolated from the companionship of other women, obliged to bear children under primitive conditions and, if they survived, raise them without benefit of convenient schools and churches. She had to endure dust storms, blizzards, droughts, blights of grasshoppers, leaking sod houses and incessant, grueling, dawn-to-dark labor in home and field.

And there was the gnawing fear of death or capture by Indians. Relatively few women suffered the latter fate, but the peril was always present. Tales of white women forced to become the concubines of "savages" sent a chill through the hearts of the hardiest pioneers.

The first order of business for most women on reaching the patch of wilderness that was to be their new home was to establish contact with the old one. Mail was agonizingly slow. Before the railroads sped up delivery, letters sometimes took half a year or more to arrive. The news was always stale but always sweet. In March of 1864, after deep snows had all but marooned the infant settlement of Bannack in southwestern Montana, Mary Edgerton happily reported to her twin in Ohio: "We have just received a package of letters. Among them were two letters from you to me, one dated July 12, the other October 5, '63. I was glad to get them even if they were not of late date."

Narcissa Whitman, one of the two missionary wives who were the first white women to make the overland journey to the West Coast, did not receive any word from her family in upstate New York until two years and five months after she had bade them goodbye in 1836. Nevertheless, she wrote letters home steadily; the very act of writing formed a bridge to the past that helped sustain her. The Whitmans and their fellow missionaries, the Spaldings, parted company after reaching the Oregon wilderness, each ministering to a different Indian tribe. But Narcissa and Eliza Spalding found a method of circumventing the slowness and uncertainty of mail delivery: they kept in psychic touch, as it were. Each morning at the agreed hour of 9 a.m., the two women, 120 wilderness miles apart, isolated themselves for a brief while to meditate on their duties as mothers and to pray for the welfare of their babies. Behind their sincere piety lay a deep need for sisterly fellowship, however tenuous.

Like many literate pioneer women, both missionaries kept journals. The daily entries served as an immediate vent of emotions, a solace for loneliness, a way of sorting out thoughts and preserving experiences. Journals and diaries provide the most intimate and detailed knowledge of how women lived in the West. The diarists seemed to sense that their lives, no matter how obscure, were part of a great historical venture that would never take place again. They wanted to record it, and they hoped thereby to capture a piece of immortality, at least among their descendants. Mollie Dorsey Sanford, an early settler in Nebraska and Colorado, asked her grandson to preserve her journal, "not from any special merit it possesses but because I do not want to be forgotten."

Most women, of course, depended on neither letters nor diaries for companionship. They did their hard daily work, looked after their menfolk and raised large families. But childbearing was at best a mixed blessing. For the Western woman, pregnancies brought special burdens—most obviously, they added to the crushing fatigues of her daily life, which depleted her physical resources dangerously. Medical help might be so far away that it could not be counted on.

In the Oregon country during the late 1830s and 1840s, Mary Walker gave birth to eight children; sometimes the doctor arrived before the babies did, sometimes he did not. Little wonder her journal took on a stoic tone: "Rose about five. Had breakfast. Got my house work done about nine. Baked six loaves of bread. Made a kettle of mush and have now a suet pudding and beef boiling. I have managed to put my clothes away and set my house in order. May the merciful be with me through the unexpected scene." Then, without any apparent pause in the account of her day, the entry concludes: "Nine o'clock p.m. was delivered of another son."

Mary Walker's case was not unusual. Charley O'Kieffe, one of nine children, described the circumstances of his birth on a Missouri River farm: "Mother herded cattle all day long in the broiling hot sun so the children could attend a Fourth of July celebration in a nearby community. The next morning around two a.m., I was born. No doctor, no nurse, no midwife, just Mother and God."

Women who gave birth on the trail could rarely count on a doctor's help. At best they had only the assistance of a female relative or friend. At worst they faced childbirth as did the teen-age Mrs. Lane from Missouri (her first name is lost to history), who went into labor on the open plains during a November blizzard, with nothing but a makeshift tent for shelter and her desperate young husband for an attendant. When the baby girl arrived, they washed her with sleet melted in a skillet, but as they were swaddling her, the mother's birth pangs came again, and a second child was born as the storm raged. The family snuggled under a pile of blankets in the wagon, and miraculously mother, father and twins all survived.

Annie Greenwood, a farmer's wife on the Snake River plains of Idaho, had to toil at household chores up to the very moment her daughter was born. She did not permit herself the luxury of complaining, but her terse recollection of the event speaks with understated bitterness: "The week Rhoda was born I cooked for fifteen men who had come to help stack hay. And in the intervals of serving them I would creep into my bedroom to sink across my bed. I was so tired. Through the bedroom window I could see the mare and the cow, turned out to pasture for weeks because they were going to have their young."

The profound, unshakable faith in God that upheld so many pioneer women forbade them to murmur against their fate. Most went no further in their questioning than Mary Walker, who wrote in her diary, "I find my children occupy so much of my time that if their

SHIP ANGELIQUE.
CALIFORNIA ASSOCIATION OF AMERICAN WOMEN.

NEW YORK, FEBRUARY 2D, 1849.

THE death of my husband, THOMAS J. FARNHAM, Esq., at San Francisco, in September last, renders it expedient that I should visit California during the coming season. Having a desire to accomplish some greater good by my journey thither than to give the necessary attention to my private affairs, and believing that the presence of women would be one of the surest checks upon many of the evils that are apprehended there, I desire to ask attention to the following sketch of a plan for organizing a party of such persons to emigrate to that country.

Among the many privations and deteriorating influences to which the thousands who are flocking thither will be subjected, one of the greatest is the absence of woman, with all her kindly cares and powers, so peculiarly conservative to man under such circumstances.

It would exceed the limits of this circular to hint at the benefits that would flow to the growing population of that wonderful region, from the introduction among them of intelligent, virtuous and efficient women. Of such only, it is proposed to make up this company. It is believed that there are hundreds, if not thousands, of such females in our country who are not bound by any tie that would hold them here, who might, by going thither, have the satisfaction of employing themselves greatly to the benefit and advantage of those who are there, and at the same time of serving their own interest more effectually than by following any employment that offers to them here.

It is proposed that the company shall consist of persons not under twenty-five years of age, who shall bring from their clergyman, or some authority of the town where they reside, satisfactory testimonials of education, character, capacity, &c., and who can contribute the sum of two hundred and fifty dollars, to defray the expenses of the voyage, make suitable provision for their accommodation after reaching San Francisco, until they shall be able to enter upon some occupation for their support, and create a fund to be held in reserve for the relief of any who may be ill, or otherwise need aid before they are able to provide for themselves.

It is believed that such an arrangement, with one hundred or one hundred and thirty persons, would enable the company to purchase or charter a vessel, and fit it up with every thing necessary to comfort on the voyage, and that the combination of all for the support of each, would give such security, both as to health, person and character, as would remove all reasonable hesitation from the minds of those who may be disposed and able to join such a mission. It is intended that the party shall include six or eight respectable married men and their families.

Those who desire further information will receive it by calling on the subscriber at

ELIZA W. FARNHAM.

The New-York built Packet Ship ANGELIQUE has been engaged to take out this Association. She is a spacious vessel, fitted up with state rooms throughout and berths of good size, well ventilated and provided in every way to secure a safe, speedy and comfortable voyage. She will be ready to sail from New-York about the 12th or 15th of April.

WE, the undersigned, having been made acquainted with the plan proposed by Mrs. FARNHAM, in the above circular, hereby express our approbation of the same, and recommend her to those who may be disposed to unite with her in it, as worthy the trust and confidence necessary to its successful conduct.

HON. J. W. EDMONDS, Judge Superior Court.
HON. W. T. McCOUN, Late Vice Chancellor.
HON. B. F. BUTLER, Late U. S. Attorney.
HON. H. GREELEY.
ISAAC T. HOPPER, Esq.
FREEMAN HUNT, Esq.
THOMAS C. DOREMUS, Esq.

W. C. BRYANT, Esq.
SHEPHERD KNAPP, Esq.
REV. GEORGE POTTS, D. D.
REV. HENRY WARD BEECHER.
MISS CATHARINE M. SEDGWICK.
MRS. C. M. KIRKLAND.

maker should see fit to withhold from me any more till they require less of my time and attention, I think I should be reconciled to such an allotment."

But unfortunately Mrs. Walker could not plan her family. Whether she welcomed her pregnancies or dreaded them, they were nearly impossible to predict, much less control. Reliable knowledge of ovulation did not begin to circulate even within the medical profession until an English doctor in 1849 published an article giving the first accurate account of the process. Before then, folk wisdom had wrongly assumed that fertility occurred in the same rhythms in humans as in domesticated animals. Many a hapless female clung to the old wives' belief that as long as a woman was nursing one baby she would not conceive another—only to add another statistic to the old saw, "One in the cradle, one at the breast, one on the way."

Contraceptive methods were primitive, disagreeable and haphazard. Access to reliable birth control information was confined largely to the wealthier, educated classes until late in the century. Such information or mechanisms as did circulate passed *sub rosa,* for to distribute or promote this material openly was punishable by law. Books on the subject were considered obscene; toward the end of the 19th Century even physicians writing on birth control were subject to prosecution. Women in the West, who were far from the centers of knowledge and isolated even from one another, were the last to learn even what limited information was available.

More than one woman desperate to avoid pregnancy resorted to the only method she knew or felt certain of—abstention. Emma Plaisted had undergone six pregnancies, three of them terminating in miscarriage, when in 1889 she reluctantly left Philadelphia to join her husband on the Dakota homestead he had gone ahead to prepare. Before her marriage she had been a professional singer and music teacher; during her husband's absence she had resumed her career and was thriving on it. Only a sense of duty—she was a minister's daughter—made her go west when the summons came from her husband. The harshness of the climate, the loneliness of the Plains, the tedium of the snowbound winters were a torment.

One of Emma's children, her daughter Elenore, began to understand as an adult something of both her parents' suffering, which she had only guessed at as a child. "Of one terrible night I have a picture branded in my memory," she wrote years later in a notebook meant for her own daughter. That night Elenore's father had been drinking from the "black bottles" he brought from town and hid under the closet. "Mother and we three children huddled into the farthest corner of one of the unplastered upstairs rooms. Horse blankets had been nailed over most of the walls, but slits of light shone between the laths. Mother had piled the furniture across the locked door.

"Downstairs there were terrifying noises—Daddy's roaring, angry voice and the sound of things crashing. Then an angry tramping up the stairs, a horse blanket being jerked aside and, through the slats, my father's face, dark red and horrible. My mother hid our heads in her skirts and talked to him. My memory of it ends there."

Elenore felt compassion for her father as well as her mother: "Years later I realized that it was the lonely prairie life, the deadly winter, the need for sex refused by my mother, unwilling to endure another pregnancy, that drove him." The strains finally forced her parents apart: within two years Emma Plaisted's health failed and the doctors told her that the Dakota climate was bad for her. She returned to the East, supported the children by giving music lessons and eventually was formally separated from her husband. After her girlhood, Elenore never saw her father again.

Perhaps even more painful than unwanted pregnancies, hazardous childbirth and the burdens of raising a large family under primitive conditions was the terrible desolation following the death of a child, particularly an only child. The bereavement of Narcissa Whitman drove her to the brink of madness. Her two-year-old daughter, Alice—the first white child born in the Northwest—was the focus and solace of her isolated life. Narcissa had carried Alice in her womb on the long journey to the West and given birth to her in the Oregon country in 1837. "O, how many melancholy hours she has saved me, while living here alone so long, especially when her father is gone for many days together," Narcissa confessed in a letter to her sister.

On the 23rd of June, 1839, little Alice fell into the Walla Walla River and drowned. Narcissa clung to

51

the dead child for four days before allowing her to be buried. "She did not begin to change in her appearance much for the first three days." she wrote to her parents. "This proved to be a great comfort to me, for so long as she looked natural and was so sweet and I could caress her, I could not bear to have her out of my sight."

The elements were an enemy to every Western mother. "We had extremely cold weather here the week before last," wrote Mary Edgerton from Bannack, Montana, in January 1864. "The mercury in thermometers after going forty degrees below zero froze in the bulb. I never knew such cold weather or anything like it. I was so afraid that the children would freeze their noses or ears in the night that I got up a number of times to see that their heads were covered. Their beds would be covered with frost. I saw their frozen breath."

On the prairie, the very grass that helped sustain life could turn into a dangerous trap for children. In Lancaster County, Nebraska, one day in 1868, two youngsters of seven and eight, a boy and a girl, decided to go looking for their brother, who was out herding cattle. In the tall grass the children lost their bearings and disappeared. For four days their distraught parents searched for them. Word came from a neighbor that the pair had turned up at his house and he had given them something to eat, but having had no reason to suspect that they were lost, he had let them go on their way. The parents finally gave the children up for dead, concluding that they had been devoured by wolves. It was only by accident that, 11 days after their disappearance, their father stumbled on them lying in the high grass, too weak from lack of food to walk. He carried them home on his back, one at a time, in relays, never letting either child out of his sight.

Catherine Blaine, the wife of Seattle's first clergyman, went to unusual lengths to keep her baby at her side during a period of danger. She had just given birth when, in 1856, an Indian uprising threatened the new community. Mrs. Blaine and her infant were rowed out to the gunboat *Decatur* for safekeeping. But the spunky Mrs. Blaine returned intermittently to her log cabin in order to catch up on her housekeeping chores. She carried her newborn child along with her. "The babe," she wrote to her family in New York, "is a month old today and I guess has been tossed about as much as a child of his age ever was. The ship is some

distance from shore so that we have to go back and forth in a small boat. He has been taken ashore some half dozen times or more. I have been off to wash and iron and do some other work. He stands it pretty well though he cries considerably from wind on his stomach, is as fat as a pig and dreadfully homely."

That last bit of levity illustrates the doughty good humor of pioneer mothers, who were, on the whole, a tough, resourceful lot, determined that their children would not only survive but also prosper in the new land. Louise Clappe, who followed her doctor husband to the California gold fields in 1851 and wrote a brilliant series of letters about her experiences, told of a woman who lost her husband on the journey west but continued on to California anyway, with her eight sons and one daughter. She was tall, gaunt and determined, like "a long-legged, very thin hen, scratching for dear life to feed her never-to-be-satisfied brood." Owning nothing in the world but the wagon and team she arrived with, she began working as a laundress, washing and ironing shirts in the open air. Her handiwork, under the circumstances, left a lot to be desired, but the men who patronized her were "too generous to be critical, and as they paid her three or four times as much as she asked, she accumulated quite a handsome sum in a few days."

Sarah Bayliss Royce was spiritual kin to that heroic washerwoman, although her intellectual attainments were of a higher order. A dedicated woman, she was determined that her children would not grow up barbarians for want of schools and libraries. After reaching California in 1849 with her husband and two-year-old daughter, she bore two more daughters and a son as the family shifted from one mining settlement to the next, finally coming to rest in a canvas tent in the Sierras.

The settlement, Grass Valley, had no adequate school, so Sarah Royce established her own. She had brought west with her in the oxcart a copy of the Bible, a volume of poetry by Milton and a portable writing desk. While crossing the desert she had found a child's storybook in an abandoned wagon. Other treasures she had picked up as she could: an encyclopedia, one or two works of history, some charts of the heavens. The Grass Valley tent even boasted a small parlor organ called a melodeon. With these as her tools, she taught

her own and the neighbors' children. Judging from one of her pupils' later achievements, she must have taught them well. Josiah Royce—the youngest member of her family, born at the Grass Valley mining camp in 1855—grew up to be one of America's most distinguished philosophers.

Many women looked at Western emigration not as a tearful, fearful obligation but as an opportunity to expand their horizons, to gain independence in a male-dominated world, to put their energies and strengths to use in ways few 19th Century women who remained in the East could hope to equal. Elinore Pruitt Rupert, for instance, discovered that homesteading in Wyoming was a broadening, liberating experience. Her letters to a previous employer in Denver engagingly chronicle the odyssey of a warm, humorous woman who made the best of the West.

Elinore Rupert was a young widow whose husband had been killed in a railroad accident. To support herself and her two-year-old daughter, she took work in Denver as a laundress and house cleaner by the day.

It was a difficult existence and she longed to escape "the rattle and bang, the glare and the soot, the smells and the hurry" of city life to "the sweet, free open" of the country. On the advice of her minister, she advertised for a position as housekeeper to a rancher— someone, she hoped, who would be able to teach her about land and water rights and help her select a homestead wisely. In the meantime she would have a place to live and some income.

Thus Elinore Rupert found herself deep in remote southwestern Wyoming near Burnt Fork, 60 miles from the railroad a week's round trip to the county seat. She was housekeeper to Clyde Stewart, a Scottish cattle rancher who spoke with a burr as thick as his wrist and played a bagpipe to cheer his bachelor solitude. "Mr. Stewart is absolutely no trouble," Elinore wrote to her friend in Denver, "for as soon as he has his meals he retires to his room and plays on his bagpipe, only he calls it his 'bugpeep.' It is 'The Campbells are Coming,' without variations, at intervals all day long and from seven till eleven at night. Sometimes I wish they would make haste and get here."

Endless round of

EMERGENCY MENDING

FEEDING THE CHICKENS

In the West isolation added a new dimension to the difficulties of housekeeping. "If I had married at home in West Virginia," lamented a frontier bride, "I should at least have had kindly neighbor women to turn to for advice, and stores where I could buy things to cover a few of my mistakes." Even when neighbors were close by, the nearest town might be several days' journey away. When the women of one Oregon community ran out of pins they used slivers of dogwood bark, and they shared a single darning needle for six months until a peddler passed through. A homesteader in Nebraska

WASHDAY

DOUGHNUTS

54

toil and making do

(*bottom right*), lucky to be living near a main road, sent her eggs and butter to town by stagecoach to be exchanged for precious commodities like thread.

Nature created other problems for Western housekeepers: a California woman had to delay fixing a meal when she found rattlesnakes coiled atop a sack of potatoes, and many a wife watched in despair as prairie dust blackened fresh laundry on the line.

In spite of the demands of domestic life, most women accepted their lot philosophically. Self-pity, said one Wyoming wife, is "the lowest state to which a woman's mind can fall."

TENDING THE GARDEN

BATHING BABY

WAITING FOR THE STAGE

FOR DESSERT

Within six weeks of her arrival, Elinore married her employer. It took her a year to confess the fact to her correspondent; she had wanted to be independent and getting married so soon "was such an inconsistent thing to do." But there was a reason. "Ranch work," she said, "seemed to require that we be married first and do our sparking afterwards."

But if she had married in haste, she had no cause to repent at leisure, remarked Elinore, "and that is very fortunate because I have never had one bit of leisure to repent in." Her situation, she wrote, was extremely comfortable: she had her own saddle horse, her own "little shotgun with which I am to kill sage chickens" and two trout streams nearby for fishing. "Well, I have

filed on my land and am now a bloated landowner," she eventually announced to her friend. The land adjoined Stewart's and the house she built — in fulfillment of the requirements of the Homestead Act — joined on to Stewart's house.

Her life now was immensely full. She bore three more children during the next three years, and in her happiness and exuberance she reached out to all those around her: matchmaking, concocting wedding suppers, planning holiday treats for lonely sheepherders, going on pack trips into the mountains.

Amid the joys of burgeoning family life and a widening circle of friends, Elinore doggedly held firm to her determination to be a homesteader, and to do it on her

Mother's cures for whatever ailed the West

As protector of her family's health, the pioneer woman confronted situations she never imagined before crossing the Mississippi. Few women came West prepared to deal with desert sunburn, rattlesnake bites or Indian arrow wounds. Even when doctors were available they were often no more knowledgeable than their patients. And most patent medicines were no more reliable than the itinerant hawkers who sold them.

In certain cases, a woman could draw upon the folk wisdom and remedies she had learned back home; Western mosquitoes, for example, proved to be as repelled by a paste of vinegar and salt as were their Eastern cousins. More often, however, a woman was guided only by her own ingenuity in concocting tonics, powders, poisons and polishes from whatever she had at hand: salt made a passable toothpaste; gunpowder was applied to warts, and turpentine to open cuts; goose grease, skunk oil

and the ever-present lard were basic liniments; medicinal teas and tonics were brewed from sunflower seeds, wild cherry bark and wahoo root.

One Wyoming woman learned to prevent snow blindness by smudging the skin below the eyes with burnt pitch pine and to thaw a frostbitten ear by applying drops of warm glycerin to it with a turkey feather. The wife of a rancher in New Mexico, following a Mexican neighbor's advice, reported curing a traveler's gangrenous arm in three days by applying toasted onion skins and plug tobacco wrapped in a warm cloth. Women learned to treat snakebite with everything from a compress of raw chicken meat to a slug of whiskey.

Townswomen coped with the aches, pains and chores of daily life in ways as homely as those employed by their sisters in the wilds. The diary kept by the women of the Gilson family of San Francisco in the early 1850s contained the recipe at right

for a combination grease- and paint-remover and shampoo. Another entry told how to soothe earache by inserting a wedge of salt pork, or puffing pipe smoke, into the ear.

Some of the remedies appear to be more dangerous than the afflictions they were supposed to cure. A teaspoonful of ammonia diluted in water and taken internally is recorded in the Gilson diary as a cure for rattlesnake bite. Other journals include such cures as a teaspoonful of sugar moistened with turpentine (for sore throat), and whiskey laced with polk root, which is poisonous, to relieve symptoms of rheumatism.

For all her inventiveness, the pioneer woman recognized the value of sometimes leaving well enough alone. To allay her son's stomachache, one woman in New Mexico routinely allowed him to go outside and lie face down in the shade all day. This remedy was successful, for reasons any mother could understand.

own. "I should not have married if Clyde had not promised I should meet all my land difficulties unaided; I wanted the fun and the experience," she told her Denver correspondent. Perhaps she exaggerated in claiming that she met her homesteading responsibilities completely without the aid of her husband. There undoubtedly was a good deal of give and take on both sides of their boundary line.

But she did relish the challenge of a multitude of farming activities. Elinore Stewart mowed hay behind a team of horses, grew large crops of potatoes and various root vegetables and experimented successfully with beans and tomatoes—in addition to making preserves and butter, milking the cows, tending and raising chickens, turkeys and children, and occasionally working in the fields. "When I read of the hard times among the Denver poor," she wrote to her friend, "I feel like urging them every one to get out and file on land. To me, homesteading is the solution of all poverty's problems, but I realize that temperament has much to do with success in any undertaking, and persons afraid of coyotes and work and loneliness had better let ranching alone. At the same time, any woman who can stand her own company, can see the beauty of the sunset, loves growing things, and is willing to put in as much time at careful labor as she does over the washtubs, will certainly succeed; will have independence, plenty to eat all the time, and a home of her own in the end." ◉

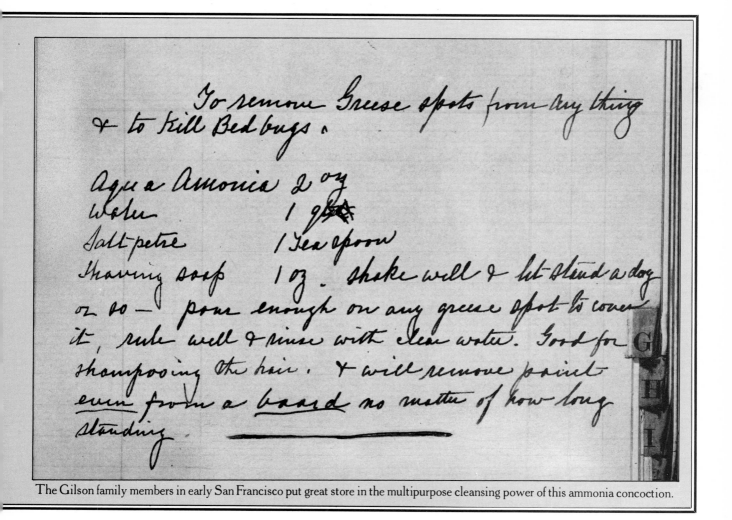

The Gilson family members in early San Francisco put great store in the multipurpose cleansing power of this ammonia concoction.

A cast-iron stove, sold for $25 in the East and $200 in some Western communities, burned coal or wood—or, in a pinch, hay.

Butter churn

A homemaker's modest appliances

A woman often set up housekeeping in her sod house, cabin or tent with three or four cooking implements, her dreams and little else. Then she forthrightly faced the unremitting challenge of "making do."

A Montana miner's wife of the 1870s who owned two kettles, a cast-iron skillet and a coffeepot considered her kitchen "well-furnished." A Nebraska homesteader moved into his schoolteacher bride's home because she had more furniture: "a small cookstove, bed, table, chairs and even a cupboard with a few dishes." Samantha Trout's cupboard in Oregon was "a box nailed to a log." And the only mirror available to women in much of the West was a bucket of water.

The rudimentary implements collected here had been either lugged from back East, built on the spot or—later in the century—summoned from the "wish book," the mail-order catalogue.

Using a time-saving fluting iron, a woman could keep ruffles in her simple calicoes.

A portable scale could weigh anything from a bucket of feed to a side of beef.

A tin lard bucket, relabeled to hold rice, also found use as a youngster's lunch pail.

Spices sold by mail order could work wonders on the monotonous frontier fare.

Real coffee and "stretchers" like rye and barley were hand ground in this box mill.

This "choke" trap helped rid a house of mice and the rattlesnakes that fed on them.

Colorado ranch hands used old packing
crates and tin sheets to build this pie safe.

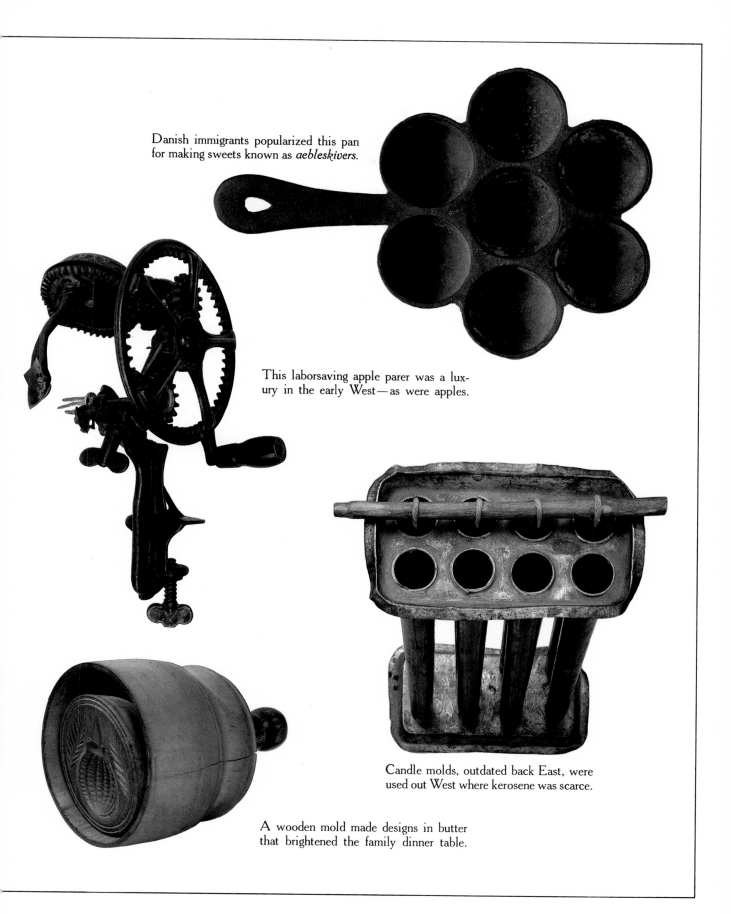

Danish immigrants popularized this pan for making sweets known as *aebleskivers.*

This laborsaving apple parer was a luxury in the early West—as were apples.

Candle molds, outdated back East, were used out West where kerosene was scarce.

A wooden mold made designs in butter that brightened the family dinner table.

The trappers, explorers and traders who were the first white men in the West often took Indian women as their mates. But with the arrival of white women in ever-growing numbers, the attitude of *laissez faire* toward mixed marriages abruptly began to disappear. No longer was it respectable for a man to cohabit with an Indian woman. White men who took Indian wives were at best tolerated as mavericks and at worst were totally ostracized. As for white women, none—it was assumed—would willingly accept an Indian as a husband. Those who were carried off by Indians and forced to live as concubines were objects of pity, curiosity or revulsion.

An Oregon man named Hauxhurst—an ex-sailor who built the first gristmill in the Willamette Valley in 1834—had been living happily with his Indian consort until female missionaries turned up in the region. Then Hauxhurst grew more and more uneasy, until one morning he gave the young woman a few presents and sent her back to her family. That night neighbors heard the distraught woman at Hauxhurst's door, "beseeching him to let her in, averring her love to him and promising to be good to him if he would let her live with him." Hauxhurst could not resist this appeal: he took her back and tried to solve his problem by legally marrying her. But this did little to satisfy the gossips: now it was held against him that he had an Indian as a wife. This was a "source for great mortification to himself and affliction to his friends," commented one observer, who added in perplexed wonder, "yet he is leading a religious life; his oldest child is at school and he takes a great interest in his children."

The plight of Indian wives and their children had its counterpart in the traumas of white women captured by Indians. For Olive Oatman, one of the West's most famous Indian captives, resuming her white identity may have been even more painful than losing it. Olive was only 13 or 14 years old in 1851 when the lone wagon of her father, a California-bound migrant who had recklessly pressed on ahead of his companions, was attacked by Yavapai Indians in a desolate part of the Gila River Valley. Everyone was felled by the Yavapai war clubs except Olive and her sister Mary Ann, aged seven, who were carried off to serve as slave laborers. A year later their captors sold them to some Mojaves, who walked the girls north to their settle-

The white woman's dread of being captured by Indians is dramatized in this 1845 painting of an Osage war dance. If she escaped scalping—and her long hair made a prized souvenir—a female captive was kept as a slave or wife.

ment on the Colorado River. Here life was slightly better: the girls received fewer beatings and were allowed to grow their own corn and melons. Then in 1853 a terrible drought struck and many in the tribe starved to death, including frail little Mary Ann.

But Olive was not alone in the world. Her older brother Lorenzo, left for dead at the scene of the massacre, had survived and made his way to safety. Immediately he had started a dogged five-year search for his sisters that at last turned up a Yuma Indian who knew of Olive's whereabouts and, for a consideration, arranged her release. In her Indian garments, her skin burned brown by the sun, Olive Oatman was barely recognizable when she reached Fort Yuma. She would not speak but sat with her face buried in her hands. It took some months before she emerged from her daze; in time she even toured on the lecture circuit and submitted to being stared at, and eventually she married. But a friend remembered that Olive Oatman was always "quiet and reserved" and that "the great suffering of her early life set her apart from the world." It was more than her suffering that isolated her. The Indians had left their physical mark on Olive Oatman: like the Mojaves she had lived among, she had been garishly tattooed on the arms, the chin and along the jawline. For the rest of her life she carried on her beautiful and somber face the emblem of her former bondage.

Another captive, quick-witted Fanny Wiggins Kelly, escaped tattooing only by pretending to faint each time her captors brought out their instruments. Later she wrote a 19th Century bestseller, *Narrative of My Captivity Among the Sioux Indians.* Some of the adventures she recounted sound like romantic fiction, but there is no question that the principal events in her story really happened.

Fanny was 19 and a bride of only nine months when the young Kellys—with Fanny's five-year-old adopted daughter, Mary, and a handful of other emigrants—set off from Fort Laramie in July of 1864. The Army had assured them that they would not have any trouble from Indians, however 80 miles westward they were surprised by a war party of 250 Oglala Sioux. Fanny Kelly's husband managed to escape (he was off chopping wood at the time of the attack) but three men were killed on the spot, and Fanny and little Mary were taken captive, along with Sarah Larimer, the other

woman in the party, and Sarah's eight-year-old son.

When Fanny wrote her famous account of the ordeal, she noted that many people had earnestly assured her they would have killed themselves rather than let Indians carry them off to heaven knows what fate. "But it is only those who have looked over the dark abyss of death," she explained, "who know how the soul shrinks from meeting the unknown future." Experience had taught her that "while hope offers the faintest token of refuge, we pause upon the fearful brink of eternity, and look back for rescue."

Fanny Kelly proved to be a winning blend of pluck and shrewdness, but at first her courage seemed the kind that makes martyrs, not survivors. As the Sioux ransacked the party's wagons, kicking aside or tossing out the things they considered useless, Sarah Larimer sent up a howl of anguish. She had planned to earn money in Idaho by taking pictures of miners, and the sight of her precious daguerreotype equipment being smashed to smithereens was too much for her. Her wails so irritated one Indian that he raised his knife and was about to put an end to her noise when Fanny rushed over and pleaded for her companion's life.

"Perhaps it was a selfish thought of future loneliness in captivity which induced me to intercede," she conceded, amazed at her own intrepidity. But a strange thing happened: the Indian turned an admiring gaze on Fanny, then took off his feather headdress and gave it to her. Only later did she realize that it was a sign of his official favor and protection. He was Ottowa, chief of the band—"very old, over seventy-five, partially blind, and very ferocious and savage looking." She would be Ottowa's property during her stay with the Oglala.

As they set off on their first night's march to the Sioux camp, Mrs. Kelly covertly shredded some pieces of paper and dropped them along the way. Then, whispering, she told little Mary to slip silently off the horse and follow the paper back to safety. Fanny said she would try to escape the same way and rejoin her. The advice turned to tragedy. Mary got away only to be caught and scalped. Fanny Kelly, detected almost immediately, was beaten and threatened with worse violence if she ever made another attempt to escape.

Fanny heeded the threat, but she was soon in trouble again for discarding the peace pipe that Ottowa had entrusted to her. It was an outrageous sacrilege and the chief decided to put her to death. She would be tied to an unbroken horse, then the horse would be whipped to a gallop and the Indians would shoot arrow after arrow into her body until their wrath was appeased. The terrified but ever-resourceful Fanny played a last, inspired card: taking out her purse, she distributed among the braves $120, all that was in it. The generosity worked magic: the Sioux put down their weapons and scrutinized the bills with intense interest, asking Fanny to explain with a show of fingers how much each was worth. They did not mention killing her again.

After this narrow escape, Fanny strove mightily to please her hosts—especially since Sarah Larimer and her child had inexplicably disappeared. Though she did not realize it at first, they had escaped.

Among the Sioux, "the brink of eternity" presented itself to Fanny Kelly with unnerving regularity. When she innocently accepted a gift of a pair of stockings from the chief's brother-in-law, she discovered that she had collaborated in a terrible breach of decorum and had inspired a feud. The irate chief revenged himself by shooting one of his brother-in-law's horses. Then it was the brother-in-law's turn to take umbrage: he drew his bow and took deadly aim at Fanny's heart. She was preparing once again to meet her Maker when salvation appeared in the shape of a young Indian who, it later appeared, was much taken with her charms. Appropriately named Jumping Bear, he leaped in and deftly snatched away the arrow before it could speed to its target. His daring act broke the deadlock. The chief gave his brother-in-law another horse, and for the moment all was well.

After the uninterrupted terror of her days on the trail with the war party, Fanny looked forward in near desperation to reaching the Sioux village. There she hoped for gentler treatment from her own sex, and to some extent she found it. But the eldest of Ottowa's six wives was a trigger-tempered shrew who sternly ruled all the other females of his household. Fanny unwittingly made the mistake of offending her. When a kindly neighbor asked the white woman over for a cooked meal, the chief decided to go along with her. At this, the No. 1 wife erupted in a paroxysm of fury. She whipped out her knife and lunged at Fanny, who took to her heels with the old woman in pursuit. Ottowa tried to intervene in the fight, "but her rage was too great," wrote Fanny, "and he struck her; at which she sprang like an infuriated tiger upon him, stabbing him in several places."

Now another combatant entered the fray. The old wife's brother, who had been watching the incident, decided it was all the captive's fault and, taking out his gun, fired six quick shots at her. He missed Fanny but one of the bullets winged the chief. When the melee subsided, they discovered that Ottowa's arm was broken near the shoulder. Mrs. Kelly was chosen to nurse him back to health, since the chief had a conviction that white women possessed special healing powers. He occasionally relieved his exasperation by pinching Fanny's arms black and blue, but that was small punishment compared with what must have befallen wife No. 1. Fanny merely reported, with studied brevity, "I never saw the wife of the chief afterward."

A series of prints illustrating Fanny Kelly's narrative, *My Captivity Among the Sioux Indians*, begins with the attack on her wagon train in July 1864. In subsequent pictures she is terrified by the behavior of her captors, uses a friendly Indian to warn the Army of a Sioux attack and finally reaches safety at Fort Sully, in Dakota Territory.

Life in the Oglala camp, by Fanny's account, abounded in such domestic brawls. Ironically Fanny, striving her utmost to survive by a steady display of obedience, cheerfulness and hard work, became a sort of role model, held up by the Oglala men as a shining example of how females should behave. She was even given the title "Real Woman," conferred on only the most admired of her sex. "The squaws are very rebellious, often displaying ungovernable and violent temper," she explained. "They consider their life a servitude, and being beaten at times like animals, and receiving no sort of sympathy, it acts upon them accordingly. The contrast between them and my patient submission had its effect upon the Indians."

Having grown fond of Real Woman, the Oglalas were reluctant to surrender her. By the time the U.S. Army discovered her whereabouts and began applying pressure for her release, she had become a coveted political prize. Independent reward hunters as well as whole tribes were eager to get their hands on her for their own gain. It was the Blackfoot Sioux who finally strong-armed the Oglalas into turning Fanny over to them. She believed, perhaps unjustly, that the Blackfeet wanted to use her as a ruse to gain entrance into Fort Sully and overwhelm that outpost. She grew desperate and is hardly to be blamed for using her charms

on Jumping Bear, the young man who had once saved her life. He visited her at the Blackfoot village to declare his love — or, in Fanny's Victorian parlance, to make "his avowal of more than ordinary feeling" — and she inveigled him into secretly carrying a letter to Fort Sully, alerting the garrison to the attack she suspected.

When Fanny was finally brought to the fort, where she was to be exchanged for three horses and a load of food supplies, a thousand mounted braves accompanied her. The garrison allowed Fanny and a few chiefs to enter, then they closed the gates quickly, leaving most of the Indians outside. The exchange was affected without hostilities and Fanny Kelly, after five harrowing months in captivity, was free at last. She never saw Jumping Bear again.

The public felt its usual voracious curiosity about a white woman taken by the Indians. As always, one question was paramount: had she been violated? Just as Olive Oatman had denied that she suffered any sexual abuse, Fanny Kelly claimed that no one had molested her either. "True, the Oglalas had treated me at times with great harshness and cruelty, yet I had never suffered from any of them the slightest personal or unchaste insult."

Although the number of women who suffered Indian captivity was quite small, they blazed in the national

consciousness as terrible proof of the irreconcilable divisions separating land-hungry white settlers from free-roaming Indian hunters. Every instance of a woman seized and held was additional justification for exterminating the Indians. However, few citizens were concerned by the outrages that some white men committed against Indian women.

Army wives were considered prime objects of Indian marauders. After all, they were asking for trouble by setting up households in the thick of Indian territory in the garrisons scattered from Fort Walla Walla in the Northwest to Fort Sam Houston in Texas. Their fears were for the most part unfounded; after 1861 there is not a single recorded instance of a woman killed by Indians at an Army post.

On occasion, Army wives were more in peril from their overprotective husbands than from the Indians. Lieutenant A. H. Wands and a company of 26, including his wife and another woman, were attacked in Sioux country in 1866. With half their number wounded, the lieutenant and his men were preparing to kill the two women and themselves, rather than face the tortures of Red Cloud's braves, when a detachment of 200 soldiers from the 18th Infantry arrived and rescued them. At Fort Phil Kearney, where Indian attacks were frequent and deadly, the commanding officer issued a standing order that if the post were overrun, the women and children were to be herded into the powder magazine and blown up. No wonder one bemused officer's wife counted her mortal peril as twofold—death or capture by Indians or death by her own friends to prevent capture.

Just such fears shook the timid breast of Ada A. Vogdes, a young bride from New York who probably would have thought twice about marrying Lieutenant Anthony Wayne Vogdes if she had known that soon after their wedding he would be ordered to the Indian frontier. She accompanied him with something less than enthusiasm, first to Fort Sedgewick in Colorado Territory and later to one of the most dangerous garrisons of all, Fort Laramie, in the heart of Sioux country. Mrs. Vogdes' journals, kept between 1868 and 1871, are the record of a rather conventional woman's change of outlook when confronted with the vivid new life around her. Having arrived at a time of relative peace, she could not help altering her opinion of the Sioux and acknowledging that they had gentlemanly qualities and even physical attractions that she had never dreamed of in her sheltered life back East.

It was her duty to play hostess to the chiefs on their frequent visits to the fort. "Yesterday Red Cloud made

Assignment to Fort Garland in Colorado Territory in 1874 meant living in this isolated outpost, 90 miles from the nearest rail depot.

his appearance at this post for the first time," she noted in her journal entry for November 5, 1868. "He and Red Leaf are the two worst Indians on the Plains. Red Cloud was the head of the party who massacred all the troops at Fort Kearney, and Red Leaf was the one who killed Gen. Fetterman, after whom the fort is called eighty miles above us." Mrs. Vogdes did not find the two leaders very intimidating; she even thought that Red Leaf had "a good fatherly looking countenance, one to whom you would go in trouble, were he in different circumstances."

But the warrior who really shattered her preconceptions was one called Big Bear. He was sociable and tried his gallant best to communicate with her. Furthermore, as she confided to the privacy of her journal, he was a superb physical specimen who wore only "leggings and moccasins, with a buffalo robe thrown over his shoulders, which exposed to view the most splendid chest and shoulders I ever laid my eyes upon."

But there were limits to a properly brought-up New Yorker's appreciation of the Indian way of life. One day Mrs. Vogdes was taken by ambulance, the enclosed wagon that was the standard mode of transportation for Army wives, to visit an Arapahoe camp. She was touched by the sight of an Indian woman bewailing the death of her son — until the tearful woman blew her nose in her hands and then wiped them on Mrs. Vogdes' dog. "I turned away in disgust," she noted with distaste, "and all my sympathy departed in this performance." Worse was yet to come: she observed other women picking nits from their children's heads and popping them "with a relish" into their mouths. This was the last straw: "I rushed to the ambulance and got inside and wished that they would have been exterminated in the twinkle of an eye, for they seemed too disgusting to be let live another day and I felt mad with the government that it should feed, clothe, and strengthen such creatures to carry on such appetites."

Troubles with Indians, real or imagined, were only a small part of the Western experience of Army women. They formed a group apart, with both the problems and

Window curtains and a flower box are evidence of a woman's decorative touch in this portrait of a Fort Garland officer's family.

A laundress and her soldier husband gather with their children in front of their log house on Suds Row at Fort Keogh, Montana. The Army arbitrarily fixed the number of laundresses at 1 to every 19½ men.

A pegged-down canvas serves as a dance floor for soldiers and their partners at a picnic. Even at isolated posts the social lives of officers and enlisted men were segregated under the military caste system.

the pleasures that their westward-moving sisters did not share. For one thing, only a single class of women—the laundresses—had any officially recognized position in the garrisons.

The wives of officers and enlisted men were described in Army regulations as "camp followers." Although the term was merely a convenient catchall for all of the civilians who moved with the troops, it was also, of course, a euphemism for the prostitutes who plied their trade in "hog ranches" located some distance away from the forts. Naturally, respectable Army women did not find it at all amusing to be grouped, even for the convenience of regulation writers, with these shady ladies. One Army wife complained that "the officers used sportively to look up the rules in the army regulations for camp followers, and read them out to us as they would the riot act!"

The commanding officer could, in fact, order any woman who was not working as a laundress off the Army post. Wives naturally resented their tenuous status but they tried their best to counteract it by making themselves indispensable to the morale and physical comfort of their men.

Even with a woman's touch, the living quarters in most frontier forts left a lot to be desired. The earthen floors were so damp that toadstools sometimes sprang up during the night and had to be swept away each morning. Insects infested the cottonwood logs of the cabins in some of the forts, and the buildings were constructed so quickly and carelessly that the wind whistled through gaps in the walls and water poured in from the roofs when it rained. One mother at Camp Cooke, in Montana Territory, checking on her three-month-old son during a rainstorm, discovered the baby almost drowning in a stream of muddy water pouring down from overhead.

Not all Western forts were that primitive. Many were without stockades and appeared to the surprised eyes of newly arrived brides like neat little villages built around a central square—the parade ground. On one side, almost always, was officers' row, a line of small cottages, usually with three or four rooms each. The

post commander's quarters were generally more impressive; he might be allotted five rooms and a kitchen—on the assumption, as one commentator wryly put it, that the higher the officer's rank the more time he spent at home. Officers' wives brightened up their quarters as best they could. Since they were a peripatetic breed who had to move constantly as their men were transferred from one fort to another, they traveled light and learned to make do with whatever came to hand. Army blankets sewn together served as carpeting, packing boxes covered with printed muslin became toilet tables and washstands, curtains blossomed out of discarded dresses and trousers.

Across the parade ground, and often hidden in back of warehouses and stables, sprawled the tents, dugouts, shanties and huts of Soapsuds Row, the abode of the laundresses and their enlisted-men husbands. The laundress as an institution in the United States Army dated back to 1802. By law she received housing, a daily ration of food, fuel, the services of the post surgeon and payment at an official rate from the officers

and men who used her services. An energetic washerwoman could earn $40 a month. Since a private's monthly income in the decades after the Civil War was $13—the Army paid for his food, shelter and uniform—it is little wonder that so many enlisted men were happy to exchange their barracks for a wife and home on Suds Row.

The laundresses were eminences to reckon with. They received the benefits of soldiers and were also subject to soldierly discipline. At least one is known to have been court-martialed for using profane language to the officer of the day. Another woman was drummed off the post under fixed bayonets after being charged with attempted murder. They have been pictured, with some justice, as a rough lot, living in Hogarthian squalor amid hordes of "shock-headed and raucous children of dubious parentage, scavenging chickens and prowling dogs." But mostly they were a congenial, large-hearted bunch who not only scrubbed away arduously on Suds Row but also often nursed the sick, mothered orphans and generally helped in times of need.

A pioneer's pride in her new state is stitched into this Map of Kansas wool quilt made in 1887 and used until 1932. The patchwork counties are identified in chain stitch and bordered by cross-stitch.

Hand-dyed homespun cotton was used for this crib quilt appliquéd with 34 stars around the word "baby." It was probably made for an infant born in 1861, the year that Kansas became the 34th state.

This pioneer variation of a standard quilt design was made by a New Hampshire woman while trailing west in 1859. Each square of the "flower basket" pattern was signed, as a memento, by a member of her wagon train. The quilt was probably assembled after its maker reached California.

PUBLIC SCHOOL.

MRS. LAURA POLLOCK
PRINCIPAL

Miss Willie Gaywood Primary Teacher

3 | The culture bearers

"School has been stopped for almost four months because a new school building is being erected," wrote Elise Amalie Waerenskjold, a Norwegian immigrant living in Texas in 1865. "It takes a very long time to complete it. God only knows how our husbands could be so indifferent toward a project which is of so very great importance to our children. In a society where the spirit of cooperation is lacking, nothing can thrive and prosper." In this one paragraph from a letter to the Old Country, Mrs. Waerenskjold summed up two major concerns of women in the West: the education of their children and the creation of civilized communities to nurture and sustain them.

Western women tackled both of these immense jobs with all the resourcefulness they could muster. Frontier schoolteachers—most of them women—met the challenge head on in back-country shacks or makeshift brush arbors on the open plain. A country schoolma'am "works the hardest and gets the nearest to no pay for it of any person I have known in a civilized and Christian land," said one writer, and teachers coping with hordes of children in crowded schools *(left)* surely would have agreed.

While these young educators—often barely older than their pupils—molded the new land's future citizens, other Western women started literary societies, libraries and discussion groups, planting seeds of culture that they hoped their children would reap.

Spilling out of a one-room school near Creede, Colorado, nearly 80 pupils have their picture taken with their teachers in 1892. In mining boomtowns like Creede, school populations often outgrew facilities.

79

A teacher smiles approvingly on her solemn students during a reading lesson in an unidentified frontier schoolhouse. For want of more scholastically inspiring art, pages cut out of a fashion magazine brighten up the roughhewn log walls.

Decked out in a stylish hat, a prim teacher named Blanche La Mont sets an example followed by her students in Hecla, Montana, for their 1893 school picture. But, hats or no hats, two boys required the company of their dogs.

Scarcely older than the "big girls" who are leading some friends through a game of London Bridge, an 1880s California teacher stands near the door of her school—a converted bunkhouse on a San Fernando Valley ranch.

A scraggly brush arbor serves as a school for these barefoot scholars in Live Oak County, Texas—which had little money to spare for education in 1887. The county courthouse, barely visible in the background, was built of adobe.

A Western blossoming of artistic talent

An art dealer in 1905 refused to believe that a painting he was exhibiting—signed simply Barchus—was created by a woman, Eliza Barchus of Oregon. "No woman painted that picture," he insisted, "so impressive in scope, with such bold strokes." He was wrong. Many women of the Old West painted with great vigor and breadth of vision, as their work on these pages clearly evidences.

By 1890 there were more than 1,100 female artists and art teachers in the West. Whether creating images with unschooled hands or applying the techniques of formal art training, they faced great odds. Their work was often belittled by the male-dominated art world. Some artists were also pioneer wives, whose chores left them little time to follow their muses. A few braved unexplored territory or subzero cold to find inspiration. An artist in the West needed plenty of courage, enthusiasm and a love of adventure as well as talent—all qualities that abounded in the women who created these pictures.

GRACE CARPENTER HUDSON

The Empty Basket (above), depicting an Indian funeral procession, and *Little Mendocino (right)*, showing an unhappy papoose, are among Grace Hudson's most famous works. Having studied at San Francisco's California School of Design in the 1880s, she began painting the Pomo Indians, a passion that thereafter dominated her life.

Western children in a mountain-rimmed playground, learning the same games as their Eastern cousins, dance farmer in the dell with a teacher. The picture was taken in 1898 from the doorway of a school near Livingston, Montana.

Hands that carried the spark of learning

When Lucia Darling arrived in Bannack, Montana, in 1863 to become the mining town's first teacher, she found the sight "not an inspiring one." Her assessment was restrained. To a young woman used to the neat, elm-lined avenues of Ohio, Bannack's muddy streets and jerry-built shacks must have been downright depressing.

She found it a place where "lawlessness and misrule seemed to be the prevailing spirit"—an observation more than borne out by others who were there. "I believe there were more desperadoes and lawless characters in Bannack in the winters of 1862, 1863 and 1864 than ever infested any other mining camp of its size," noted one Montana pioneer. "Murders, robberies, and shooting scrapes were of everyday occurrence in daylight as well as at night." A woman writing from Bannack the year Lucia arrived added that there "are times when it really is unsafe to go through the main street, the bullets whizz around so. What do you think of a place where men openly walk with shotguns, waiting to shoot some one against whom they have a grudge, and no one attempts to prevent it?"

But the business of a schoolteacher is to foster hope for the future, and Lucia Darling saw a brighter side of Bannack. "Into this little town had drifted many worthy people who unbendingly held firm to their principles of right," she wrote later. "Parents were anxious to have their children in school and it never was known when there came a cry from the children that some school ma'am did not rise up in response." In Bannack it was the spirited Lucia who rose up in response to the children's need for education—the cry, of course, having come from the parents rather than the youngsters. In October she took over a small room in her uncle's log dwelling and began teaching her first 20 pupils.

The next year, 1864, began inauspiciously enough in Bannack with the hanging of the sheriff, who—while in office—had led a gang of highwaymen in the ambush and killing of some 100 miners. But that summer, the town built a crude little cabin to serve as Lucia Darling's schoolhouse. Bannack was still hardly a model community, but Lucia took pride in being on the front line of civilization. "The school was not pretentious," she wrote later, "but it was in response to the yearning for education and it was the *first.*"

Lucia Darling was only one of thousands of women—not all, or even most, of them schoolteachers—who arrived in the West bearing books and other tokens of culture and their notions of what a civilized society should be. Women were still hampered by restrictive ideas of what was and was not suitable for a lady. But frontiersmen regarded women—and Western women regarded themselves—as heralds, preservers and arbiters of culture and tradition. This was, in the life of the West, a pretty wide niche and women filled it admirably.

Lucia Darling opined that pioneer women had "a more lasting influence than was realized at the time." Their impact was certainly lasting, but it was also often immediate and pronounced. In the early 1880s all the businesses of Grand Junction, Colorado, shut down at 2 p.m. every Sunday so that the entire populace—some 300 souls—could gather to hear the town's first schoolteacher, Miss Nannie Blain, read and discuss the Bible. When Miss Blain had said her piece, the shops and saloons of the rowdy cattle town reopened for the rest of the day.

Although the results were not always so readily apparent, women arriving in the West quickly set

---

"The Schoolmistress," as portrayed in an 1853 book, *Western Characters,* was a beady-eyed old maid. In truth, most Western teachers were young and marriageable.

Lucia Darling, the first schoolteacher in Montana, was a firm believer that "a higher civilization has always followed closely in the footsteps of the women pioneers."

about trying to re-create the noblest aspects of the communities they had left behind. Wherever and whenever women settled, schools, churches, libraries and charitable societies soon blossomed. No aspiration seemed too high nor any undertaking too daunting: one woman in the 1850s founded one of the first universities on the Pacific Coast.

Women also started organizations solely to enrich their own and other women's lives and, in the West's agricultural areas, they infiltrated men's groups. One observer in the 1870s noted approvingly that a "certain ratio of lady members" in farmers' granges on the Plains resulted not only in welcome "social intercourse amongst the members" but also in "a good library, an organ or piano, a microscope, botanical collections, &C." Thus, hard-working farmers were taught that "books, flowers and pictures have as real a value as threshing and mowing machines."

As hard as Western women worked to refine and enlighten their husbands, they worked even harder on their children. They put great faith in God and education, but not necessarily in that order. While early American colonists used to raise the church as soon as

living quarters had gone up, 19th Century frontier communities often built themselves a schoolhouse first. Whether on the plains of Nebraska or in a gold camp in California, newly arrived mothers promptly saw to their children's education, either by sending them to school or by giving them lessons in their own homes if no school was close enough.

Mary Luella Nesmith White of Nebraska was one pioneer woman determined that her children would not grow up barbarians. "Before coming to Dundy County," she wrote of the move her family made in 1887, "I had expressly stipulated how important having school was, and that there must be school privileges for the children." But the two schools in the district turned out to be several miles away and on the other side of the river, "so that meant no school for us that winter."

That is, there would be no formal schoolhouse schooling. While her husband constructed their sod house and barns, Mary White said, "I considered it my duty to teach the children. This I did in accordance with my time and resources." With the children gathered round, "often I held a school book in one hand and wielded a white-wash brush with the other. At other times I propped a book in front of the wash-tub while I rubbed soiled clothes on the wash-board with both hands. Sometimes I was to sit down comfortably in a chair and teach my rebellious child who seemed determined not to learn. I was just as equally determined she should, so after while she, in cheerful spirit, continued her lessons day by day."

In subsequent years, the children of Mrs. White's growing family went to school, although they were "forced to get across the river as best they could. Sometimes they waded, sometimes in winter they had to jump from cake to cake of ice. Sometimes they mired down in quicksand. Two makeshift foot bridges proved to be unsafe and unsatisfactory." Years later this single-minded mother acknowledged dryly that her children's school memories "may not be altogether happy." But she added with pride, "we reared eight children to maturity, of these six were daughters, and all six enjoyed teaching school!"

Before such prairie-reared daughters grew up to take on the job, schoolteachers out West usually came from the East, and they were not always received with total delight. Nannie Blain giving her Sunday Bible

In Nebraska a schoolma'am had to earn a
certificate like this—or a lower-ranking
"third grade" certificate—by taking exams and showing "good moral character."

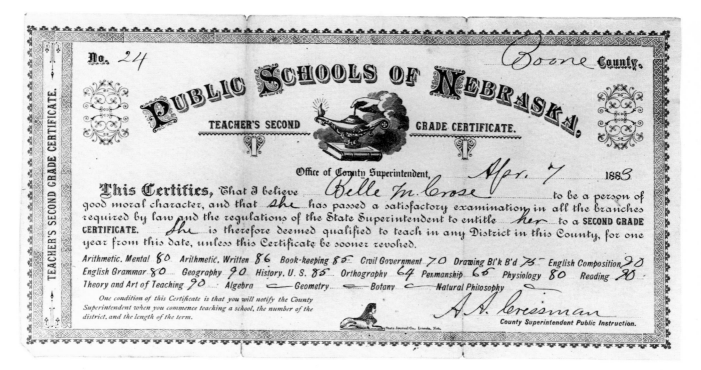

lessons might be respected in Grand Junction, but in
some parts of the West any intrusion that even hinted
of the old hierarchy of class and caste left behind in the
East could be resented, as Sarah Raymond found.

With her widowed mother and brothers, Sarah arrived at Virginia City, Montana, on September 5,
1865. Though the Raymonds had fallen on hard
times, they were an educated family; 25-year-old
Sarah had been a schoolteacher in Missouri. Sarah
wrote that on her first day in Virginia City, she encountered a miner's wife who lived near the Raymonds'
campsite. When the woman asked her how she
planned to make a living, Sarah said she hoped to teach
school. "I presume I did not make a very favorable
impression," Sarah wrote, "for after I came back to
camp she called across the street to her neighbor—so
we could hear what she said: 'Some more aristocrats.
They didn't come here to work. Going to teach school
and play lady,' with great contempt in her voice."

Sarah Raymond was able to laugh to herself at the
notion that teaching was not work, but that she could
be accused of "playing the lady" by teaching represented a complete turnaround from attitudes a generation
earlier, when, by the code of the times, a lady did not
work for wages. Until after the Civil War, even teach-

ing had been considered a man's profession. But men
had abandoned the field for better-paying work, and the
doors of the schoolhouses were wide open.

One woman who deserves much of the credit for
enhancing the prestige of women in classrooms, and
encouraging the westward flow of schoolma'ams to
take the place of men, was Catharine Beecher. The
daughter of Lyman Beecher, the famous minister, she
became deeply concerned about education on the ex-
panding frontier. Her widely read *The Duty of American Women to Their Country,* published in 1845,
charged that men were deserting the schoolroom's
"humble, unhonored toils," leaving millions of children
to grow up uneducated, a situation as dangerous to a
young democracy as it was deplorable. "It is *woman*
who is to come in at this emergency and meet the
demand," wrote Catharine Beecher, "woman, whom
experience and testing has shown to be the best, as well
as the cheapest, guardian and teacher of childhood, in
the school as well as in the nursery."

Indeed, cheapness, rather than skill, was often the
primary factor that recommended females to impoverished school boards. Certainly the several hundred
Eastern women who heeded Catharine Beecher did
not expect to make their fortunes in the frontier class-

room. The contract between Maud Geller and School District No. 22 of Wheeler County, Nebraska, for example, arranged that in return for teaching school "in a faithful and efficient manner" for three months, "said School District agrees to pay Maud Geller the sum of $25.00 per month for said services, and to keep the schoolhouse in good repair, and to provide the necessary fuel." Meager as this seems, the average Western teacher earned more per month than her counterparts elsewhere in the country. However, frontier schools were rarely in session for more than three or four months a year, and teachers had to scramble to keep themselves going with other jobs or live 12 months on four months' salary.

Many teachers were no more than 15 years old when they took their first jobs. These young pioneer women in their one-room schoolhouses were the backbone of education in frontier America in the late 19th Century. Between 1870 and 1900, Nebraska and Kansas could boast some of the highest literacy rates in the country, even though few of the teachers there had had any formal training (they only had to pass cursory examinations on basic subjects to receive their certificates), and some hoped to learn as much as they taught.

"Well, here I am at my first school," wrote Anna Webber, who kept a diary of her initiation into teaching in Blue Hill, Center Township, Kansas, from May through July of 1881. "I realy wander if I'll like it. I wander how I'll get along." Spelling and grammar were not Anna Webber's strong points, but in spite of this her journal is a remarkable document, a kind of quiet, written memorial to all the dedicated young women who taught in the West. From it emerges a picture of a determined and resourceful girl overcoming uncertainty and frustration to bring some kind of education to a passel of "scholars" on the lonely plains of Kansas.

"My anticipations are great," she wrote. "I am going to try to make rapid improvement. The Supt gave me *such a desperate* look while I was reading at the examination, that I resolved to 'learn to read loud.' I think if hollowing will do any good I'll overcome that fault entirely. I have a scholar that is some deaf, and I've 'hollered' and talked today until my throat aches."

Being away from her family was a great trial and her homesickness was often wrenching. "I am among entire strangers, not knowing before I came here a single person," she wrote. Once she kept a futile watch for two days in hopes that "some of my folks would come to see me." But she resolutely bucked herself up against loneliness with exhortations to "study and try to make myself worthy of their respect."

Chief among her frustrations was the lack of even the most rudimentary equipment in her school. "There is no benches, seats, black board or writing desks," she recorded the first day. "I am now sitting on the floor with my paper on 'the Teacher's chair.' For seats we have two boards placed on rocks. I think if I had things more convenient I should like teaching very much."

Toward the end of May she was "in *hourly expectation of those seats* and black board," but although she got a table on May 30 ("The table makes it seem like a different place"), no seats arrived until after July 4. "We commenced school that morning on a new scale," the teacher exulted. "The children was nearly as proud as I was, and acted like a mess of little crazy bedbugs."

Anna seems to have had few disciplinary problems, except for a chap named Charlie Anderson. "It seems impossibility for him to learn the alphabet," she wrote of Charlie. "He is such a careless, lazy little rascal. He seems to take no interest whatever in trying to learn. I don't know what to do with him." When the weather got sultry, however, the behavior of all her charges deteriorated. "I dread warm days. The pupils are so restless and unquiet, and have poor lessons."

By the time Anna's three-month teaching stint was nearing its end, she had grown into her job. "There is only nine days more of school," she wrote on July 16. "It seems a long time since I left home, but it does not seem like I had taught nearly three months. The school-house looks so nice that I hate to leave it."

But she had scant time for melancholy in the madhouse of preparation for the "entertainment" that traditionally closed out the term. Parents would come to see what their children had learned, and a teacher's reputation could be made or broken according to how well her pupils performed. "We are learning our 'pieces' and making preparations for the last day," she wrote, "and it keeps me just a 'humping,' I have to learn my own and teach the children theirs. If I can only keep my self controll, I think I can get along all right. But I tell you it is going to be a severe trial. I may as well begin practic-

In spite of rigorous exams coming up, two young students giggle while conspiring over lunches taken from a lard pail and an old tobacco tin. The girls were attending a frontier school in Oregon logging country.

Indians who led the way in women's education

Cultural attainment on the frontier was not the exclusive aspiration of white settlers; the first school for the higher education of women west of the Mississippi was founded in 1851 not by pioneers but by Cherokee Indians, who saw education as the road to equality with whites.

To those settlers who viewed Indians as dangerous barbarians, the Cherokee National Female Seminary in Park Hill, Oklahoma, must have seemed a remarkable phenomenon. The seminary's original building was a classic two-story brick structure complete with Doric pillars. The students, Cherokee girls aged 14 and older, dressed like white women—many were descended from intermarriages—and studied subjects such as "mental arithmetic," philosophy, chemistry, and Latin. During their four years at "Fem. Sem.," they also had Bible lessons, physical culture classes and up to an hour of housekeeping chores daily.

In light of Cherokee history, it was not surprising that the Indians provided a high standard of education for their women. Despite harsh treatment from the federal government, which had forcibly driven the Cherokees to Oklahoma from their original homeland in the southeastern United States, the tribe over the years had assiduously adopted what it consid-

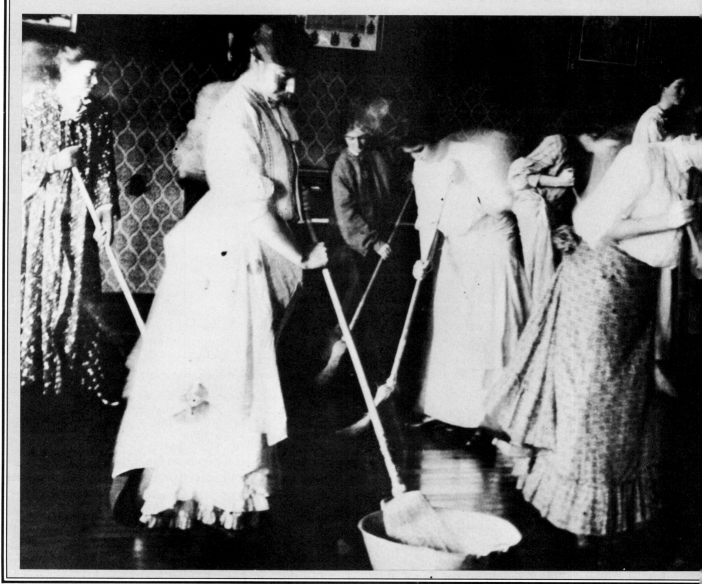

ered the best elements of the white man's culture. The founding of the school—and that of a male seminary at the same time—followed an intellectual tradition that already included the invention of a Cherokee alphabet, the printing of books and newspapers in their own language and tuition-free elementary education.

To recruit the first teachers for the new women's school, two Cherokee leaders traveled to Mount Holyoke Female Seminary in Massachusetts. That school had a reputation for the kind of rigorous academic training the Indians wished to emulate. "Fem. Sem." soon attained a high standard of educational excellence, but the school was plagued by troubles. Five years after the seminary opened, financial difficulties forced the tribe to close it. Reopened after the Civil War, it was destroyed by fire in 1887. The determined Cherokees constructed a new, larger building *(below, right)* at Tahlequah, Oklahoma Territory, their tribal capital.

There the school flourished until 1907, when Oklahoma became a state and swallowed up the Cherokees' political and educational institutions. But even then "Fem. Sem." did not disappear; it was absorbed into a state-run coeducational institution that eventually became Oklahoma's Northeastern State College.

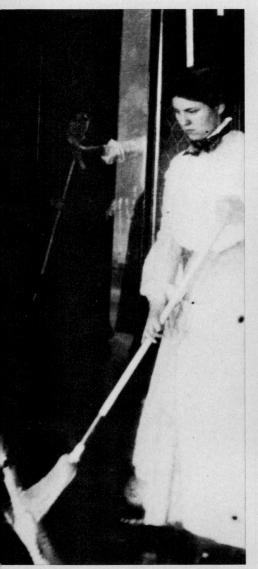

Following a curriculum that mixed practicality with academic excellence, students *(left)* scrub a floor at the Cherokee Female Seminary. The seminarians standing before the building that was the school's second home *(above)* reflect the mixed ancestry of many Cherokees.

A white woman tries to convert an Indian to Christianity in this romanticized 1857 painting by Tompkins Matteson. During the mid-19th Century there were more than double the number of women as men attached to the West's Christian missions.

to her destination. In her journal she recalled that neither she nor her sister "could find Trinidad on the map except in the island of Cuba. So we concluded that Cuba was my destination."

She soon learned, however, that her Trinidad was a little mining town in southwestern Colorado. Two men among the friends who came to see her off at the Steubenville station drew her aside, their faces very serious. Earnestly they tried to warn her of the dangers she faced in crossing the Plains. "Travelers are sometimes snowbound for two weeks, and you are alone. This, though, is not the greatest danger to you. Your real danger is from cowboys." Sister Blandina looked at them blankly. "You do not seem to grasp our meaning. No virtuous woman is safe near a cowboy." Seeing that they were not making the slightest impression, they gave up. "Why should snow or cowboys frighten me any more than others who will be traveling the same way!" Sister Blandina wrote.

Twelve days later, she remembered those words and trembled. She had come by train to the terminus in Kit Carson, Colorado Territory, and from there she rode a construction train until the tracks gave out. Now began a 24-hour stagecoach ride that tried even the jaunty Sister Blandina. There were no other passengers on the stage, and she could see nothing, for every flap covering the windows was fastened down, doubtless against the cold. Jerking up and down over the ruts in a springless carriage, for the first time Sister Blandina began to have "indefinable fears." Noon came, suppertime came, midnight came, but at each stop for fresh mules, Sister Blandina could eat nothing. The cowboys were preying on her mind.

At the midnight stop, out of the blackness she heard footsteps approaching. Her heart pounded. "You will have a traveling companion for some miles," announced the stage driver. By lantern light she could make out a tall, lanky man wearing a broad-brimmed hat and carrying a buffalo robe. While Sister Blandina sat transfixed, he got in, took a seat beside her and spread his robe over them both. The door closed; they were in total darkness. There was not the slightest doubt in Sister Blandina's mind that this was a cowboy, and with every throb of her temples the Steuben-

In austere Sunday garb, Presbyterian missionaries approach a potential convert at an Apache camp in Oklahoma in 1898. Scandalized Christian women aimed to coax Indians away from their love of gambling, dancing and exchanging wives.

ville warning hammered through her brain: *No virtuous woman is safe near a cowboy.*

"I made an act of contrition—concentrated my thoughts on God—thought of the Archbishop's blessing, 'Angels guard your steps,' and moved to such position as would put my heart in range with his revolver. I expected he would speak—I answer—he fire. The agony endured cannot be written. The silence and suspense unimaginable. Suddenly from out the darkness I heard: 'Madam!' 'Sir?' 'What kind of a lady be you?' 'A Sister of Charity.' 'Whose sister?' 'Everyone's sister, a person who gives her life to do good to others.' 'Quaker like, I reckon?' 'No, not quite.' "

The tone of the cowboy's voice had by then told Sister Blandina she had nothing to fear. Indeed, before their ride ended she had extracted from him not only his life story but also a promise to write to his neglected mother the minute he got off the stage and to visit her as soon as possible. "To think that this lubberly, good-natured cowboy had made me undergo such mortal anguish." Sister Blandina had cleared one psychological hurdle and would soon have to surmount another.

The first glimpse of her new home revealed some dugouts in the foothills. "A fainting feeling came over me," she confessed, "as I looked at what I would have thought were kennels for dogs." Sister Blandina realized why she had not found "this small pebble" on the map. The town consisted of little more than two streets, each about two blocks long, with only one house that to her Ohio-trained eyes looked like a residence. Some 75 humble adobe dwellings stood apart in a section called Mexican Hill. Early in 1870 three Sisters of Charity had arrived from Cincinnati to found a parochial school, called the Academy. When Sister Blandina stepped off the stagecoach, roughly three years later, she found that the Sisters had also begun the territory's first public school, and it was Sister Blandina's assignment to be the public schoolteacher.

Before her first day was out she was reviewing her Spanish, in order to converse with the local Mexicans, and encouraging the other nuns in the little convent to join her. "Here, if you have a largeness of vision," she wrote, "you find the opportunity to exercise it; if a cramped one, the immense expanse of the plains, the

A religious builder mixing faith and mortar

Mother Joseph close to her 70th year.

Striding purposefully among the carpenters and laborers at a building site, the tall, sturdy nun was clearly in command. With a hammer hanging like a six gun from the belt of her habit and a saw in her hand, she shouted instructions, occasionally stopping to help a workman. This scene was repeated many times during the 46 years that Mother Joseph served the Church in the Northwest.

The 33-year-old nun arrived in the Oregon country, a Protestant stronghold, in 1856 from the Sisters of Providence headquarters in Montreal. She won the hearts of Northwesterners by financing, designing and building most of the region's first hospitals and schools, which she opened to people of all faiths.

To raise money for the 30-odd major institutions she established from Oregon to Alaska, Mother Joseph braved Indians and outlaws on her "begging tours" in the wild. She usually arrived at mining camps and Army posts on paydays, accompanied by younger nuns who could charm the men out of their money.

Armed with carpentry skills learned from her father, a Montreal carriage maker, Mother Joseph insisted on high-quality work. Once, finding a chimney that had been improperly constructed, she personally tore it down and rebuilt it overnight. Half a century after her death in 1902, the American Institute of Architects saluted Mother Joseph as "the Pacific Northwest's first architect."

St. Mary Hospital, built by Mother Joseph in Astoria, Oregon, in 1885, was a remodeled hotel plus a new wing with tower.

solid Rockies, the purity of the atmosphere, the fault-lessness of the canopy above, will stretch the mind toward the Good." She had decided on her personal plan of action for life in the West: she would do whatever presented itself and "never omit anything because of hardship or repugnance."

Trinidad's location only 12 miles from the New Mexico border made it a rendezvous point for outlaws dodging from one territory to the other. Justice was haphazard: before the circuit court judge arrived on his periodic pilgrimage from Denver, anyone confined in the adobe jail had usually burrowed his way to freedom. The result was that lynch law prevailed.

One day, one of Sister Blandina's older pupils reported, white-faced, that his father was about to be lynched. For some reason he had shot a young Irishman with a gun loaded with poisonous tinshot. The father was in jail, but perhaps not for long: men had already posted themselves in a line between the jail and the dying man's room. The moment death came, they would tap the school bell three times as a signal for the mob to assemble, then advance on the jail, drag out its inmate and hang him.

Sister Blandina decided she must intervene, and she quickly worked out a scheme. First she sent word to both assailant and victim, asking if each would agree to her plan. When both said yes, she obtained the astonished sheriff's ready consent. Then ensued one of the strangest scenes ever witnessed in the West. From the jail emerged the trembling prisoner, with the tiny, black-clad nun on one side and the six-foot-four-inch sheriff ("a person with plenty of reserve strength, and on the *qui vive* to use a portion of it") on the other. While the would-be lynchers looked on, the incongruous trio proceeded in silence to the wounded man's room. There, by preagreement, the miscreant asked his victim's pardon. Then, at the sight of the wounded man's ugly leg, already swollen with the poison that would kill him, the prisoner blurted out a genuinely heartfelt plea to be forgiven. "I forgive you, as I hope to be forgiven," replied the victim, "but the law must take its course." The door was wide open so that those outside could hear. "Yes, the law must take its course—not mob law," repeated Sister Blandina.

The scheme worked. When nun and sheriff walked the prisoner back, no one tried to snatch him from their grasp. Three days later, when the young man died, the mob did not reassemble. The prisoner was held safely for trial by the circuit court, which convicted him of manslaughter and sentenced him to 10 years.

In 21 years in the West, Sister Blandina won support from whatever community was her home. In Trinidad, taking what she called "an opportunity to carry out a test on the good in human nature," she managed to build a new schoolhouse despite the fact that the Sisters of Charity had no money. Borrowing a crowbar, Sister Blandina clambered onto the roof of the old, airless adobe shack that had served as a school, and she began to pry loose the bricks, tossing them onto the street, one by one. The first passerby exclaimed "For the love of God, Sister, what are you doing?" and promptly dragooned six men into helping with the demolition of the old building. Materials for the new one were donated by town merchants as well as by more distant families—including one from 60 miles away that had a daughter at the school.

After Trinidad, she spent many tireless years in Santa Fe and Albuquerque. "I do not know what fatigue feels like," she would say, confessing to her journal. "It is stimulating to meet emergencies."

The more one learns about early Western women, whether they were Sisters of Charity, young school-ma'ams or determined mothers, the more striking is the vigor and endurance they evidenced. Certainly they needed both these qualities in full measure, first to get across the plains and then to provide for their families. The astonishing thing is that they had so much energy left over to share with their communities.

One woman well supplied with vigor and endurance—and a strong sense of community—was Tabitha Moffat Brown. Sixty-six years old and weighing scarcely a hundred pounds when she made her journey from Missouri to Oregon in 1846, she lost virtually everything she owned en route and arrived in the Willamette Valley with not much more than the clothes on her back. That she survived this odyssey is remarkable enough, but Tabitha Brown went on to found one of the earliest institutions of higher learning on the West Coast, Pacific University—and she did it even though she began life in the West with a grand total of six-and-a-quarter cents. "God had a work for me to do," she would write some years later, "and had seen fit to use me to accomplish His own purposes."

Tabitha Brown had been a widow for 30 years and was still teaching school in St. Charles, Missouri, when her eldest son, Orus, began to organize a wagon train heading for Oregon. Rhapsodic over the country he had found in the Willamette Valley, he persuaded his mother and sister to join him on his trek to "Paradise." Even his uncle John Brown, a 77-year-old retired sea captain, insisted on coming along. The company left Missouri in April of 1846, and all went smoothly until they had passed Fort Hall, in what is now southeastern Idaho.

"Then we were within 600 miles of Oregon City, if we had kept on the old road down the Columbia River," Tabitha wrote later to her brother. "But three or four trains of emigrants were decoyed off by a rascally fellow, who came out from the settlement in Oregon, assuring us that he had found a near cut-off; that if we would follow him, we would be in the settlement long before those who had gone down the Columbia." The idea was appealing and the man proposed to charge only a small guide fee per wagon. It was now August.

Her story of the next four months is, considering the situation, calmly matter-of-fact. The guide "robbed us of what he could" and left them to the mercy of Indians, wild animals and sometimes impassable terrain. "Our sufferings from that time no tongue can tell. We had sixty miles of desert without grass or water, mountains to climb, cattle giving out, wagons breaking, emigrants sick and dying, hostile Indians to guard against by night and by day. We were carried south of Oregon hundreds of miles into Utah Territory and California; fell in with the Clamotte"—that is, Klamath—"and Rogue River Indians; lost nearly all of our cattle."

She rode through the Umpqua Mountains in three days "at the risk of my life, having lost my wagon and all I had but the horse I was on." After many miles of "mud, rocks, and water up to our horses' sides" and brushes with starvation, on Christmas 1846, Tabitha entered a Methodist minister's house in Salem, Oregon, "the first I had set foot in for nine months."

The harrowing phase of her adventures was over, but now that she had reached her destination, how was she to make a living in this "young man's country"? First, in return for taking charge of the minister's house

and family ("his wife was as ignorant and useless as a heathen goddess"), Tabitha and Captain Brown were able to board there through the winter.

"For two or three weeks of my journey down the Willamette," she wrote, "I'd something in the end of my glove finger, which I supposed to be a button. On examination at my new home in Salem, I found it to be a six-and-one-fourth cent piece; this was the whole of my cash capital to commence business in Oregon.

"With it I purchased three needles, traded off some of my old clothes to the squaws for buckskin, and worked it into gloves for the Oregon ladies and gentlemen. This cleared me upwards of $30."

The following October she visited her son, Orus, who had settled on the West Tualatin Plains, at a place now known as Forest Grove, and there she met the Reverend and Mrs. Harvey Clark, missionaries from New York, who had been in Oregon since 1840. Invited to spend a few days with the Clarks, she was soon like part of the family and was pressed to stay the entire winter. When word came that scores of emigrant children were being orphaned on the trail, Tabitha—who had been keeping busy, but not busy enough to suit her—said to Harvey Clark, "Why has Providence frowned on me and left me poor in this world? Had He blessed me with riches as He has many others, I know right well what I should do. I should establish myself in a comfortable house and receive all poor children and be a mother to them."

The Reverend Clark "fixed his keen eyes upon me and asked if I was candid in what I said. 'Yes, I am.' 'If so, I will try with you and see what we can do.'"

Clark provided the means for her to start a school for orphans. Thus, in the spring of 1848, at the age of 68, Tabitha Brown "found all things in readiness for me to go into the old meetinghouse and cluck up my chickens the next Monday morning." The first place in the territory where children could live and study, Tabitha's school grew quickly as parents from the settlement sent their children there. Those who could afford it were charged a dollar a week per child. Tabitha—who had "a well-educated lady from the East, a missionary's wife," as teacher—managed the school with tremendous efficiency. She worked the first year for nothing. By 1851, Tabitha Brown had 40 in her "family" at Tualatin Academy, as her school was called.

When the arrival of women brought family life to Virginia City, Montana, the town first established a school *(near left)*. Only then, having provided for the education of the children, did Virginia City construct its first church *(above and at far left)*.

Finally, in 1854, the territorial legislature altered the academy's charter to provide for the creation of another institution: Pacific University. Both the academy and the university thrived side by side under the inspiration of this doughty woman, who came to be known to all her charges as "Grandma" Brown. In December 1854 she wrote to her brother about making a trip back East. "Our President and Board of the University are anxious that I should try the undertaking; they say I could do more and have a greater influence on the rich nabobs and charitable Christian people in the cities than any of the trustees here.

"The idea of a lady seventy-four years of age coming from the Pacific coast on a mission from Oregon for the sake of obtaining funds for the institution which has sprung up by her being the first to make the proposition! It is not impossible that I may try the trip yet."

Tabitha Brown never did return to the East, but as she wrote to her brother, "I have labored hard for myself and the public and the rising generation. I now have quit hard work and live at my ease." And well might she: she owned several lots in town, a house that she rented out and cows that she "let out for their milk and one-half the increase." Besides her time and labor she had contributed several hundred dollars to the school she was so instrumental in founding. All this she accomplished "by my own industry and good management independent of my children, since I drew six-and-a-quarter cents from the finger of my glove."

The university founded on Tabitha Brown's concern for children is simply one example of the way Western women molded independent pioneers into communities of citizens who looked after each other. In San

Literary triumph of a New Yorker in Leadville

Before 1876 it would have been beyond Mary Anna Hallock's wildest imaginings that critics would one day hail her as "an authentic voice of the West" for her novels about life in rough mining towns. She had never been West then; she was not even a writer, but a successful illustrator enjoying a sophisticated life in New York. Her drawings had appeared in *Harper's Weekly* and *Scribner's Monthly*, and many books.

In 1876 she married Arthur Foote, a young civil engineer who yearned to seek his fortune in the West. Mary Foote abandoned her cultivated Eastern existence for the raw environment of New Almaden, California. Homesick, she sought to retain her ties to the East by prolific correspondence with Richard Gilder, editor of *Scribner's*, and his wife, Helena. Mrs. Foote's letters includ-

ed such vivid descriptions of New Almaden and its inhabitants that Gilder decided to piece some of them together and publish them as an article in his magazine.

Given this encouragement, Mary Foote began selling articles and short stories, often illustrating her own pieces. But it was not until she and Arthur moved to the silver-mining town of Leadville, Colorado, that Mary's writing career began to truly blossom. Out of that tough and exciting boomtown came her first novels and her reputation as a Western writer of note.

Mrs. Foote's best-known novel, *The Led-Horse Claim*, was a romance played out against the background of the Leadville silver boom. Though the Footes moved to Idaho and eventually returned to California, Leadville remained Mary's chief font

of material. Though her books colorfully described the roughhewn denizens of frontier towns, they did not realistically present the brutality and squalor that was often part of Western life. "I could not get that sort of realism into my stories for I was one of the 'protected' women of that time," she later said. "As much of Leadville life as my husband thought I could 'get away with' he told me."

But she described with poignant conviction the subject she knew best: the plight of the West's many transplanted women. In a novel called *The Last Assembly Ball* she wrote: "When an Eastern woman goes West, she parts at one wrench with family, clan, traditions, clique, cult and all that has hitherto enabled her to merge her outlines—the support, the explanation, the excuse, should she need one for her personality."

Francisco one day in 1853, Mrs. A. B. Eaton opened her door to a stranger, a young woman who tearfully poured out what had become an all-too-common tale in that gold rush city. After a lengthy journey around Cape Horn, the girl had arrived that afternoon, expecting to be met by her brother. But no one was waiting for her, nor was there any message. Perhaps her brother had never received her letter. Or worse, maybe he was dead. She had been wandering the street in despair when she had seen Mrs. Eaton's kind face at the window, and now she was appealing for help.

Because of this encounter Mrs. Eaton founded the Ladies Protection and Relief Society, dedicated to rendering "protection and assistance to strangers, to sick and dependent women and children." Formed by churchwomen of various denominations, the society quickly became one of San Francisco's most prominent

charitable organizations, providing an orphanage as well as a temporary shelter for destitute women or those suffering a sudden run of misfortune.

This kind of public-spirited endeavor was neither more nor less than what was expected of women—with their "finer natures" and sensibilities. But many Western women, isolated on farms or in mining camps, burdened with the care of house and children, longed to join their sisters in a different kind of association, in which they could exchange whatever ideas they pleased without regard to a charitable purpose. Until the last quarter of the 19th Century, however, this aspiration met scorn. "There was little sympathy with organizations of women not expressly religious, charitable, or intended to promote charitable objects," wrote one woman in 1898. If women gathered for some purpose other than "the making of garments, or the collec-

In an illustration by Mary Foote for *Century* magazine, a homesteader scans the sky for wild geese with which to feed his family.

tion of funds for a church," their motives were suspect.

Nonetheless, in the decade after the Civil War, a "new form of social and mental architecture" appeared: a woman's club, with no specific philanthropy in mind. Championing this heresy in the West was Caroline M. Severance, who had earlier founded the New England Woman's Club of Boston, which pledged itself only to "a womanly interest in all true thought and effort on behalf of woman, and of society in general, for which women are so largely responsible." Moving to Los Angeles in 1875, Caroline Severance found "a town of great possibilities and many attractions, but with the few advantages of a frontier town." She "plunged ardently" into the business of adding to these advantages, and the first woman's club in Los Angeles was formed three years later.

If Los Angeles in 1875 was a frontier town, some of the prairie and mountain states were like the dark side of the moon. "Time has been required to develop the gentler elements out of the nebulae which float in at the making of new States and Territories," wrote Jennie June Croly in her 1898 *History of the Woman's Club Movement in America*. "To the women of the new West the modern missionary has been the club." Mrs. Croly's exhaustive volume chronicled the deeds and personages of the hundreds of woman's clubs springing up all over the country.

Nebraska: "The women are in earnest. A wave of enthusiastic desire for social and mental improvement is sweeping through the small towns and remoter districts, and needs only the help of women in more favored localities to become an intellectual crusade."

Victor, Colorado: "Delegates to the State federation in Pueblo, from that portion of the Cripple Creek district which calls itself the 'greatest gold camp on earth,' certainly seemed to deserve some credit for creating a centre of refinement and higher civilization in the midst of their discouraging environment."

"Discouraging" was probably too mild an adjective to describe Cripple Creek, Colorado, where 13 intrepid women formed a Woman's Club in 1896. A tough mining town that had its heyday in the 1890s, Cripple Creek was the home of the famous madam, henna-haired Pearl de Vere *(pages 144-147)*.

In spite of the raucous atmosphere of the town, the Woman's Club of Cripple Creek gave musical concerts, formed a "well-trained chorus, equal to any other amateur chorus of the same size in America," and by the year 1898 was forming "the nucleus of a public library." Further, about the same time that Cripple Creek lost Pearl de Vere to an overdose of morphine, "a delightful programme was carried out one day by the brilliant young artist, Charles Partridge Adams, of Denver. His address was illustrated by a number of beautiful pictures which he displayed and described. It was the first art exhibition that Cripple Creek had ever enjoyed," wrote Jennie Croly, adding, "Where there are no theatres, no lectures, and but little social life, a club like the Woman's Club is an infinite blessing."

For all Caroline Severance' intentions that woman's clubs not be tied to or defined by philanthropic or charitable deeds, most clubs took up some cause. Civic efforts ranged from protecting shade trees to "placing anti-expectorant notices" in public places. But the most widespread club activity, reflecting the unvarying bond between these women and the worlds symbolized by books, was the establishment of libraries.

Libraries—and librarians—had a kind of ripple effect in their communities that was often hard to measure, but California-born author Jack London was one who felt compelled to acknowledge the influence one librarian had on his life. In December 1906, he wrote her a letter about it: "The old Oakland library days! Do you know, you were the first one who ever complimented me on my choice of reading matter? Nobody at home bothered their heads over what I read. I was an eager, thirsty, hungry little kid—and one day at the library I drew out a volume on Pizarro in Peru (I was 10 years old). You got the book and stamped it for me; and as you handed it to me you praised me for reading books of that nature. Proud! If you only knew how proud your words made me! For I thought a great deal of you. You were a goddess to me. I didn't know you were a poet, or that you had ever done such a wonderful thing as write a line."

The woman to whom London wrote this tribute was Ina Coolbrith, who was then 65 years old, suffering from rheumatism that often kept her bedridden and struggling to regain some security after her home had been destroyed in the earthquake and fire that had devastated San Francisco in April. Born in Nauvoo, Illinois, in 1841 and named Josephine Donna Smith

Lady with camera in the wilds of Montana

British-born Evelyn Jephson Cameron came to Montana on her honeymoon in 1889 and later returned to produce an outstanding photographic record of the state's early days. She and her husband, Ewen, an avid naturalist, were so taken by Montana's primitive beauty that they made their home there.

An accomplished photographer, Mrs. Cameron—called "Lady" Cameron by neighbors impressed by her genteel manners and British accent—lugged her bulky camera equipment about the countryside, photographing people and places. Proud of her work, Mrs. Cameron also relished her reputation as the first woman in all Montana to ride astride a horse, rather than sidesaddle.

In her ranch house near Terry, Montana, Evelyn Cameron examines a batch of photographs that she developed in her own darkroom.

Evelyn Cameron's pictures preserve many candid vignettes of pioneer existence, as well as the adventurous flavor of her life with her husband, Ewen *(above)*, photographed playing with their pet wolves, Tussa and Weecharpee. At top right, a farm family prepares a meal for field hands. Below, a young Montana couple finds refuge from the harsh pioneer life in their snug kitchen. And on the brilliantly sunny day that Mrs. Cameron photographed a heavily laden chuck wagon lumbering across the prairie *(bottom right)*, she included—perhaps intentionally—her own shadow.

Beaming proudly, women of Monte Vista, Colorado, show off their new public library. Begun in 1885 by the Women's Literary Club, the library was moved to the new building from a member's home.

(her uncle was Joseph Smith, founder of the Church of Jesus Christ of Latter-day Saints), Ina Coolbrith emigrated to California with her family in 1851.

She grew up in Los Angeles and published her first poems there under the name "Ina," a pet name derived from Josephine, at the age of 15. After a brief and unhappy marriage and the death of her only child, Ina moved to San Francisco, adopted her mother's maiden name, Coolbrith, and attempted to begin a new life. She was 21 years old and subject to bouts of melancholy that often infused her poetry, but within two years—while holding down a teaching job—she had

begun publishing in the *Golden Era* and the *Californian,* two of San Francisco's literary weeklies.

In the fall of 1864 she met Bret Harte and began a union that soon put her at the center of literary society. When Harte began editing the *Overland Monthly* in 1868, Ina was a "constant contributor," according to poet Charles Stoddard who, with Harte and Miss Coolbrith, formed the "Golden Gate Trinity."

Indeed, life for Ina Coolbrith in the late 1860s and early 1870s was full of promise. Charles Stoddard recalled, "Her muse was speedily and cordially recognized in the best quarters, and, in later years when on a

flying visit to the Atlantic sea-board, Whittier and many another master-singer welcomed her fraternally."

But a series of family crises, culminating in the death of her older sister, put a tremendous burden on Miss Coolbrith's shoulders. By 1874, her mother and her orphaned niece and nephew were dependent on her for support. Occasional poems in the *Overland Monthly* were not enough to provide food and shelter. (Much later an enthusiastic fan would gush, "Oh, Miss Coolbrith, our whole family just lives on your poems!" Ina Coolbrith replied, "How nice. That is more than I was ever able to do.") So, in September 1874 she began 20 years as librarian at the Oakland Public Library.

Later Ina Coolbrith would declare, "I am prouder of being the first public librarian in California than I am of being the first woman author, for I think the public libraries have been a greater help to the people." Nevertheless, other Western women felt the touch of Ina Coolbrith, librarian, as well as the inspiration of Ina Coolbrith, author. One of these was Mary Austin, who captured the desert country of southern California in *The Land of Little Rain,* a slim volume of sketches that became an acknowledged Western classic, remembered "a tall, slow woman, wearing an expression which I think she must have acquired crossing the plains as a child, the look of one accustomed to uninhibited space and wide horizons. She had a low, pleasant voice; now and then a faint smile swam to the surface of her look, and passed without the slightest riffle of a laugh; and she was entirely kind and matter of fact with me. She told me how to prepare my manuscripts and advised me to see the *Overland* editor."

In 1919 the state legislature gave Ina Coolbrith the honorary title of Loved Laurel-Crowned Poet of California. Her acceptance speech, while acknowledging her pride and gratitude, also recognized the fact that she had never been prolific. "By me poetry has been regarded not only as supremest of arts, but as a divine gift, for the best use of which its recipient should be fitted by education, time, opportunity. None of these have been mine. The 'higher education' was not open to my sex in my youth, although, singularly, I was the first woman to furnish a commencement poem to any university, which I did at the request of the faculty of the University of California; and in a life of unremitting labor, 'time and opportunity' have been denied. So my meagre output of verse is the result of odd moments, and only done at all because so wholly a labor of love."

Several years earlier, when a San Francisco newspaper asked her what she would do with a million dollars, Ina Coolbrith answered that she would "provide training schools in which girls and women wage-earners might be educated and thoroughly fitted for some occupation, that would insure their freedom from slavery." The poet continued, in words that called to mind the thousands of women who came West, carrying their precious books and melodeons across the plains and deserts, determined to preserve the best of the worlds they had left behind: "And, as woman does not live by bread alone any more than man, I would have in connection therewith libraries and reading rooms, lectures and music, that the mind and heart might be fed as well as the body, and life be endowed with its greatest humanizing and moral influences, hope and happiness."

A Western blossoming of artistic talent

An art dealer in 1905 refused to believe that a painting he was exhibiting—signed simply Barchus—was created by a woman, Eliza Barchus of Oregon. "No woman painted that picture," he insisted, "so impressive in scope, with such bold strokes." He was wrong. Many women of the Old West painted with great vigor and breadth of vision, as their work on these pages clearly evidences.

By 1890 there were more than 1,100 female artists and art teachers in the West. Whether creating images with unschooled hands or applying the techniques of formal art training, they faced great odds. Their work was often belittled by the male-dominated art world. Some artists were also pioneer wives, whose chores left them little time to follow their muses. A few braved unexplored territory or subzero cold to find inspiration. An artist in the West needed plenty of courage, enthusiasm and a love of adventure as well as talent—all qualities that abounded in the women who created these pictures.

GRACE CARPENTER HUDSON

The Empty Basket (above), depicting an Indian funeral procession, and *Little Mendocino (right)*, showing an unhappy papoose, are among Grace Hudson's most famous works. Having studied at San Francisco's California School of Design in the 1880s, she began painting the Pomo Indians, a passion that thereafter dominated her life.

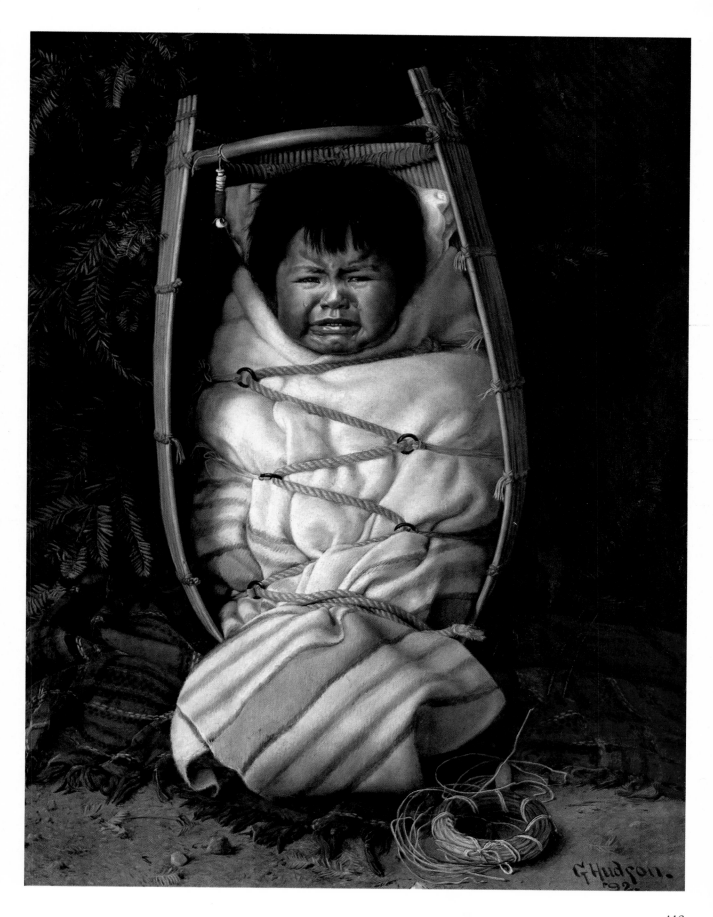

MARY ELIZABETH ACHEY

Among Mary Achey's earliest Western works are a view of a Colorado mining town, Nevadaville *(right)*, and a sketch of a frontier military post *(above)* she drew while accompanying her Army husband. When their only daughter died from fever, Mary irrationally blamed her spouse. She left him and spent the rest of her life moving around the West. Legend said she carried her daughter's remains with her for a year before allowing burial. She painted continually and was probably the most prolific woman artist in the West from 1860 to 1885, when she died at 53.

HELEN TANNER BRODT

The beauty of actress Lily Langtry is immortalized in this
pastel study that Helen Brodt rendered in the 1890s. A
noted portraitist, Mrs. Brodt moved from New York to California in 1863, and she painted there until she died in 1908.

EMMA EDWARDS GREEN

The state seal of Idaho, designed by Emma Green in 1890
and approved the following year, was the first in the nation to
be created by a woman. After studying art in New York, Mrs.
Green was drawn back to Idaho by her love of the West.

ELIZA BARCHUS

An overcast sky casts a pink glow around Mount Hood, seen here in one of Eliza Barchus' thousands of paintings of that Oregon prominence. A widow who had young children, she successfully supported her family by painting and teaching. After 1885 her pictures earned such fame that she was known as "The Oregon Artist."

The most impressive establishment in Glendale, Oregon, in the 1890s was the Hotel Clarke, owned and operated by Catherine Clarke, a widow. After starting the business with her husband, John, Catherine managed the hotel while he prospected in Montana and ran it after his death.

4 | On the new career trail

Pushing a load of freight down a wilderness trail behind a team of obstreperous oxen was one of the least appealing occupations in the West. That any woman would volunteer for such a job was remarkable; that a few, like Arizona Mary *(right),* apparently relished the work is a measure of the range and mettle of the women who found ways to support themselves while opening up the new country.

Not every Western woman who worked for pay had the unusual stamina—or the leather lungs and salty vocabulary—required of a bullwhacker. According to the 1870 census, most working women in the West, in fact, pursued familiar occupations such as laundress, cook or teacher—as well as one profession completely ignored by the census, prostitution.

But whether dance-hall girl or lawyer, working women shared many traits. They were adventurous, as they proved first by heading west and again by entering the male-dominated work force. They were stubborn and unsentimental, yet they could be unstintingly generous to anyone in need. They were resourceful, often able to toss together an imaginative salad of a business from unpromising ingredients—and turn a profit with the concoction. Most of all, they were tough-minded. "When I saw something that needed doing, I did it," one woman said, and her life proved it: she had been both a hotel operator and a miner.

A bullwhacker known as Arizona Mary drove her eight yoke of oxen the way a man did—by filling their ears with curses and by cracking a whip over their heads.

Milliner Emma Gibbs *(center)* is flanked by a clutch of her satisfied clients in this turn-of-the-century photograph of her Reno, Nevada, shop. Miss Gibbs not only created new hat styles but also remodeled old frocks and did elaborate embroidery, a skill she advertised as "art needlework."

Ollie Beers cheerfully digs an irrigation ditch on the Colorado farm that she and her four sisters ran for their invalid father. After his death the five daughters successfully converted the 480-acre spread into a 60-cow dairy operation.

Around the turn of the century, women prepare peaches for drying in the California sun. Such seasonal work provided farm wives and daughters with money that helped alleviate the crop-to-crop cash shortage that plagued small farmers.

Typesetters prepare an edition of the *Kansas Workman,* a weekly newspaper founded in 1883. Women were often preferred for arranging the tiny pieces of lead type, inky work that placed a premium on dexterity—and sobriety.

Earning a living in a man's world

"This is the only country that I ever was in where a woman recd anything like a just compensation for work," wrote a San Francisco seamstress around 1850 to a friend back East. "I am perfectly contented and have no wish to return." Nor had many other Western working women who, between 1840 and the turn of the century, earned a living—and sometimes much more—working at a variety of jobs that were well beyond the hopes, or even the aspirations, of most women back East.

True, most working women labored at familiar tasks—as laundresses, cooks, teachers, housekeepers. But many surged into businesses and elbowed their way into professions that were traditionally a man's province. Women became shopkeepers, restaurateurs, brewers, pawnbrokers, barbers and photographers. One particularly enterprising woman in California built and ran a factory that produced 50,000 orange crates a year, and in Montana a woman matched her muscles against oak and iron as a wheelwright.

In a region saturated with men who were sick to death of the sound, sight and smell of themselves, women of small talent and great courage could make a living on the stage. Really good actresses and singers—whether home-grown or from the East or from Europe—were huge box-office draws. In 1853 tickets to Lola Montez' San Francisco debut sold at auction for up to $65. Men fell over one another to pay out their gold dust for a turn around the floor with a dance-hall girl or to spend an hour with one of the many prostitutes who, after domestics, may have made up the second-largest group of working women in the West.

As the years passed and the rough edges of the frontier began to erode, women entered the professions in increasing numbers. They became not only teachers but also doctors, dentists, lawyers and journalists. By 1890 the West was, comparatively speaking, a font of opportunity for women. There were almost five times as many actresses per female capita as there were in the East, nearly four times as many women lawyers and twice the number of doctors and journalists.

Yet few of the women who undertook these jobs had come west originally for the chance to work. Groups of unmarried women gathered to migrate west together, drawn primarily by the prospects of finding husbands. And the prospects were excellent: most were married shortly after their arrival. The majority of wives devoted most of their energy to making their homes as comfortable as possible under primitive conditions. Wives who managed to work for pay gave up their earnings to the head of the household and were applauded for it. One woman in the California gold fields must have worked herself to death to receive the following praise from an admiring male at her funeral: "Magnificent woman that, sir. A wife of the right sort, she was. Why she earnt her old man nine hundred dollars in nine weeks, clear of all expenses, by washing. Such women ain't common, I tell you. If they were a man might marry and make money by the operation."

Any married woman faced the possibility of suddenly being called upon to support herself and her children. Frontier violence and a life of physical hardship combined with scarce and sometimes quack medical care could abruptly deprive wives of their husbands. And if death itself did not intervene, the depressing realities of frontier life all too often killed marriages. Divorce could be had for the asking in much of the West. In Dakota Territory one woman obtained a divorce just 10 days after a bill on her behalf was introduced to the legisla-

The work of Mrs. Clinton Lasley, a professional photographer, is advertised in this portrait of herself *(left)* and a friend, taken in her California studio during the 1890s.

These 1853 entries in the diary of California laundress Chastina Rix emphasize her work, but also show her interest in prohibition.

"Thursday 25.
Ironing fine shirts all day. Alfred went to the mission

Friday 26. Ironing again— In all this week I have ironed sixty shirts. 35 starched one & 25 plain besides lots of other clothes & I have made twelve dollars by my labor. Went to a temperance discussion this evening at Mr Briggs church. They are discussing the Maine law here. this required considerable courage with their hundreds of rum selling places open in their faces. The rum seller was on the ground to defend his side

Saturday 27
Baking &c. Calls from Mr. Smith and Morris—"

ture. One Easterner inquiring out West about his estranged wife discovered she had divorced him six months earlier without bothering to notify him.

Widows and divorcées in the East might be sheltered by relatives after losing their husbands, but Western women who moved away from familial security had to look out for themselves—and in most cases Western society approved of women who could do it.

Making a living on the frontier was always a challenge; industry and versatility were the keys to survival, and many women worked at more than one kind of job to make ends meet. Julia Shannon, an aspiring daguerreotypist, advertised to San Franciscans in 1850 that "those wishing to have a good likeness are informed that they can have them taken in a very superior manner, and by a *real live lady* too. Give her a call, gents." Later the same year, Mrs. Shannon announced her availability as a midwife, proudly listing 12 physicians as references.

In Los Angeles at about the same time, an athletically inclined woman who ran a small restaurant picked up extra income by offering her customers lessons in swordplay. So formidable was she with the rapier that only one man was reported to have bested her. The frontier village of Walla Walla, Washington, in the 1850s harbored Madame Bauer, a remarkable linguist

who spoke French, German, Italian and Spanish and was a scholar of Hebrew and Latin besides. But to supplement her earnings from language lessons, Madame Bauer also taught plain and fancy needlework.

Few Westerners looked down on these women who, by choice or necessity, worked for pay. About 1880 Nannie Alderson left Union, West Virginia, where "you had to have your pedigree with you to be accepted anywhere," to visit her aunt who lived in Atchison, Kansas. She was amazed by the social openness she found on the Plains. "What impressed me most," she reported, "was the fact that a girl could work in an office or a store, yet that wouldn't keep her from being invited to the nicest homes or marrying one of the nicest boys. This freedom to work seemed to me a wonderful thing."

"A 'biled' shirt lasts a good while," reported Horace Greeley in the 1860s. "I noted some in use which the dry, fine dust of that region must have been weeks in bringing to the rigidity and clayey yellow or tobbaco stain hue which they unchangeably wore during the days that I enjoyed the society of the wearers."

Nevertheless, an occasional clean shirt was a genuine pleasure, so a gold mine of dirty clothes, a richer lode than many a prospector ever found in the hills,

In 1860, when Clara Brown moved her laundry 40 miles from Auraria, Colorado, to Mountain City, blacks were not allowed in public coaches. So Clara paid a prospector to drive her as his "hired help."

awaited any woman who could tolerate long days of boiling and ironing. Men in general—and miners in particular—refused to do laundry. Not only was it "women's work" but a man could hardly concentrate on prospecting while washing his shirts.

In 1854 a woman wrote to her mother from Horse-shoe Bar, Miner's Ravine, California: "There is a lady lives close by me that takes in washing and she makes from 15 to 20 dollars a week washing when she has all she wants to do." Clara Brown, a freed slave from Kentucky, charged 50 cents apiece for washing those crusty shirts that Horace Greely marveled at. Investing her money in land, she saved $10,000 in a few years, which she used to help other exslaves find work in Colorado and to mount a successful search for a daughter who had been sold away from her years ago.

Laundry service came so dear in the gold fields that miners near San Francisco resorted to a drastic solution. "Washing is still $8.00 a dozen," a miner lamented over the price of laundry done locally, "and the consequence is, large quantities of soiled linen are sent to China to be purified—and the practice is now becoming general. A vessel just in from Canton brought 250 doz. which were sent out a few months ago." The pokey service apparently did not matter as much to the miners as saving a few dollars.

Laundering was only one of the ways an enterprising woman could strike it rich in the gold fields. In 1849 Luzena Wilson arrived in Nevada City, California, with her husband and two toddlers. The family had little money, and while her husband split logs into shingles to build a waterproof shelter, Luzena set about making the family fortune. "I cast my thoughts about me for some plan to assist in the recuperation of the family finances," she told her biographer-daughter more than 30 years later. "As always occurs to the mind of a woman, I thought of taking boarders." Nevada City already had one boardinghouse, a canvas-roofed affair that charged a dollar a meal. The competition only aroused the businesswoman in Luzena, and she decided to set up a rival establishment.

"With my own hands I chopped stakes, drove them into the ground, and set up my table. I bought provisions at a neighboring store, and when my husband came back at night he found, mid the weird light of the pine torches, twenty miners eating at my table."

Twenty men forked over $20, and Luzena's husband soon joined her as a partner in the prospering enterprise. The money poured in, enough to build a small house and then to enlarge it a room at a time to accommodate an ever-increasing number of guests. Soon the hotel housed between 75 and 200 boarders, each paying $25 a week. With the money rolling in, Luzena Wilson unshouldered some of the work. "I became luxurious," she recalled, "and hired a cook and waiters. Maintaining only my position as managing housekeeper, I retired from active business in the kitchen." In her spare time Luzena sewed for the miners and put aside some $500, which she loaned out in booming Nevada City at 10 per cent interest—per month.

Within six months the Wilsons had opened a store, and Luzena estimated the worth of their buildings and goods at $20,000. One night a fire all but wiped out Nevada City, including the Wilsons' fine hotel. "The remnant of our fortune consisted of five hundred dollars, which my husband had in his pockets and had

131

The most impressive establishment in Glendale, Oregon, in the 1890s was the Hotel Clarke, owned and operated by Catherine Clarke, a widow. After starting the business with her husband, John, Catherine managed the hotel while he prospected in Montana and ran it after his death.

133

Katrina Murat's eyes still sparkle with high spirits near the end of her flamboyant hotel-keeping career. She was as kind as she was extravagant; a Denver oldtimer said that she would give a man a meal when he "hadn't the price of a sandwich."

neglected to put away, and with that sum we were to start again." They did. Not long after, the Wilsons established another hotel, which became the nucleus of Vacaville, California.

Starting over from scratch was a fate common to businesswomen on the frontier, whether they were wiped out accidentally like Luzena Wilson or through their own profligacy like Katrina Murat, who by some accounts was the first white woman in Denver. In 1859 Katrina, her second husband, Henri, and a partner named David Smoke opened the Eldorado, the first hotel in Auraria, a mining camp that was absorbed into Denver the following year. A typical boomtown flophouse, the Eldorado was built of cottonwood logs, measured 17 by 20 feet and had a floor of leveled earth. Inside, a few pieces of crude furniture stood around a fireplace of sticks plastered together with mud. Beds were nothing more than piles of buffalo robes and a few blankets, but they were never empty; cold, weary miners occupied them in shifts around the

clock. Katrina worked as cook, chambermaid and laundress. Smoke was the janitor and handyman. Henri tended bar and barbered the miners.

Henri also was charged with seeking prospective guests for the hotel; to spy them out, he sat for hours in a squat log tower atop the Eldorado. Attired in tails and topper, he scanned the prairie for approaching wagon trains. Spotting one, he would jump on his pony and ride to greet it, a high-styled advertisement for his inn. Among the guests he corralled was Horace Greeley, who reportedly had difficulty sleeping at the Eldorado "due to the promiscuous firing of pistols."

The Eldorado was a peculiar enterprise for the Murats, both of whom had tasted the good life in Europe. Katrina, the polished daughter of a well-to-do German vintner, had emigrated from Germany with her first husband in 1848. Henri appeared to be black-sheep royalty; at least, he called himself a count, professing to be a nephew of Joachim Murat, the Frenchman whom Napoleon I had installed as king of Naples. When the Count met Katrina, he was working as a dentist in San Francisco and she had $75,000 in her pocket, an inheritance from her first husband. Honeymooning in Europe, the Murats spent almost all of Katrina's stake, setting the pattern for a boom-and-bust life that they would follow for the next two decades.

Henri and Smoke reputedly drank up most of the Eldorado's profits, and the Murats moved on. In another part of Denver they established a combination saloon and barbershop. It featured Katrina's cooking and boasted the town's first lunch counter. The reviews were raves: "Such noodles, such coffee bread, such wiener-schnitzel, such steaming kraut, such piping pot roasts, such herring salad were never before that day or since served to hungry men," wrote one effusive customer. But this venture turned out to be transitory, as did various others. When times were flush the Murats traveled, twice to California, and four times to Europe, where they concentrated on the fashionable spots with alluring casinos. When they ran out of money they returned to the West to start another business.

In the mid-1860s Katrina and the Count opened the spectacular Continental restaurant in Virginia City, Montana. An establishment for connoisseurs, the Continental featured costly champagnes and wines and homemade ice cream. A Swiss cook and an assistant

Cassie Hill's certificate as a Wells Fargo agent is a rarity. Records show that by 1900 only three such awards had been given to women.

helped Katrina turn out her delicious and expensive fare. Her pies, for which she was especially famous, cost two dollars or more. In a few years the Murats had accumulated about $60,000 and headed back to Denver. Katrina carried their gold concealed in small buckskin bags sewn to the inside of her voluminous skirt. The ruse foiled road agents, but the bags rubbed Katrina's legs raw and left them permanently scarred. By 1876 the money had been spent, and here the see-saw saga finally came to an end. The Murats never rose to affluence again. Henri died penniless in 1885; Katrina lived on until 1910 as a recluse supported by the Pioneer Ladies Aid Society.

Turning domestic work into a business had great appeal to women since they could capitalize on their long apprenticeship in the home. Others, however, paid equal attention to their husbands' work, and frequently

took it up themselves. During the years Cassie Hill's husband ran the Wells Fargo depot in Roseville, California, she learned the intricacies of telegraphy, transferred funds back East, ran a freight office and even assayed gold offered in exchange for coin. When her husband died in 1885, Mrs. Hill took over the office and operated it successfully for 23 years.

Mrs. Clinton Lasley, the wife of a photographer, learned her husband's trade by watching over his shoulder in the studio. In 1896, when he became intrigued with pharmacy and opened a drugstore, Mrs. Lasley took charge of the photography business herself. Photography was an attractive occupation. As a feminist handbook of 1894 observed, it was a calling "for which the training requires less time and money than almost any other that has as good pecuniary results. As for the demand, good work will always create it." Perhaps, but Abbie Cardozo found she needed an edge

Residents of Randsburg, California, show off a theater, built in 1896 when the mining town was less than a year old. Within the wood front and canvas walls were "a tinny piano, dance floor and small stage."

to compete successfully with several other studios in the small town of Ferndale, California, in the 1890s. She traveled to San Francisco where she learned hairdressing, and when she returned, offered a premium to her clientele: "Mrs. A. E. Cardozo of the post office gallery is back," ran a newspaper advertisement. "The very latest in the line of photography. No extra charge to patrons for hair dressing."

A photographer who styled hair, a woman butcher in Los Angeles who loaned money, milliners, candy-store owners and dressmakers—these women and thousands of others like them toiled to satisfy the daily needs of their communities. Yet other women avoided the workaday world entirely, earning their livings as entertainers when the shops were locked up tight and the cows shut safely in the barn.

The women who played frontier theaters—singers, dancers and actresses—had a head start on the road to success simply because they were women; in much of the West, that alone was enough to attract a crowd. The novelty of the experience overshadowed the often-primitive quality of entertainment in makeshift surroundings. Some troupers performed on the street for stray dimes, or a saloonkeeper might sponsor the talent, allowing the use of his bar as a stage.

But there were limits to what even isolated miners would accept from unskilled performers, regardless of sex. Antoinette Adams, for example, discovered that singing for miners in Virginia City, Nevada, could be at once embarrassing and rewarding. Antoinette was far from young and not much to look at, and she could barely croak a note, but the miners listened politely to her, the first woman to grace their stage. After the second song, however, one of the audience rose and proposed, to unanimous approval, that they should endow "Aunty" with enough money for a well-deserved—and immediate—retirement. A shower of silver followed the resolution.

Talented performers, on the other hand, could acquire a following that stayed loyal for years. Lotta Crabtree first appeared on stage when she was eight years old in Rabbit Creek, California. From the outset, Lotta was an uninhibited performer who endeared herself to audiences. In her debut she danced a jig and sang adult love ballads. As a teenager in the 1860s she was baring her legs and smoking on stage, unladylike con-

137

Daredevil women defy gravity in a poster advertising their act at the Bird Cage Theatre in Tombstone, Arizona, in 1889. Not long after that performance, one of the women plunged to her death when clamps on her shoes slipped from holes bored into the ceiling to suspend her above the stage.

return home. Helena, however, was determined to stay in America with her husband and return to the stage. Of her decision to resume her career as an actress, Helena wrote: "Call it vanity, if you like; I prefer to call it pride or ambition. Some people in Poland know of my intention of appearing on the English-speaking stage, and I hear they already predict my failure. I left Poland as the leading lady of the Warsaw Theatre; I will return as an acknowledged star of foreign stages."

Learning English was Helena's first step toward American stardom. A generous young San Francisco woman devoted entire days, without pay, to coaching the actress in the intricacies of pronunciation. She also studied her new language by memorizing the parts of Juliet and Cleopatra in Shakespeare's dramas. She enchanted an influential San Francisco lawyer, Edward Salomon, who secured an audition for her with John McCullough, manager of the California Theatre. He hired her immediately to star in a popular play of the day. Though her debut had its uncertain moments, Helena was pleased with herself. "A curious feature of this, my first performance in English, was that I was not in the least nervous. Even when my veil caught fire from the foot-lights, I had enough presence of mind to put it out immediately." Success in San Francisco led to an appearance in New York, a tour in London and, just as she had predicted three years earlier, a triumphant return to her native Poland.

As the theatrical tastes of Western audiences matured, the theater became increasingly formal. Fewer people attended to be entertained than to be seen in a cultural setting. No longer could raucous advice be shouted from the back row. Doffing one's coat in an overheated theater could evoke such scorn that many a man sweltered rather than endure the disapproval.

There had always been establishments in the West, however, where a man's comfort was of prime importance, where he could remove his coat and relax among women who offered a kind of entertainment not to be found at the opera house. It was these women whom men turned to for less constrained diversions.

Prostitutes and dance-hall girls stormed mining camps along with — and sometimes doubling as — laundresses and cooks. They were gold diggers in their own way, selling intimacy in varying degrees to a market of nearly limitless demand, financed by glittering dust. As long as a town prospered, the women stayed; when a gold strike waned, they moved on. Some women entered the profession from respectable marriages. Others deserted it for a husband. The girls were often young — in Kansas the typical prostitute was in her late teens and rarely worked past her early twenties. A very few became wealthy as madams of elegant "sporting houses." Some fell victim to the hazards of their trade: venereal disease, a crude abortion, too much drink, an overdose of laudanum, an assault by a jealous man.

Women sold companionship in a variety of settings. In saloons and theaters, performers — jig dancers, singers, the chorines — were often required to mix with the customers after their work on stage. Such women sometimes made enough money from performing and from a share of inflated drink prices so that they felt no pressing economic need to sell sexual favors. Society considered them a little less soiled than the prostitutes who lived solely by renting their bodies.

The position of women of easy virtue in frontier society changed with the times. Initially welcomed by hordes of woman-hungry men, they later were ostracized by the townsfolk — men and women alike — who were seeking to emulate Eastern respectability.

Nevertheless, the oldest profession continued to prosper. Hurdy-gurdy houses — as dance halls were known — offered their clientele women dressed "in the finest clothes money can buy," wrote Thomas Dimsdale, a chronicler of 19th Century Montana. "The music suddenly strikes up, and the summons, 'take your partners for the next dance,' is promptly answered by some of the male spectators, who, paying a dollar in gold for a ticket, approach the ladies' bench and — in style polite, or otherwise — invite one of the ladies to dance." The dancers could become wealthy. They were showered with money and gifts, and they might spend $700 or more on an elegant gown.

Complaints against hurdy-gurdies centered about the vast amounts of money squandered there nightly. But city fathers shrewdly detected a way to make the dance halls, if not citadels of morality, at least pillars of financial support. Wrote Sidney Edgerton, Montana's territorial governor, to the first Montana legislature: "In Oregon the dancehouses have to pay a license of $100 per month. Why not in Virginia City? Let those who want to dance pirouette at will, but, until some other less necessary subject for taxation be found, let the Hurdy-Gurdy houses pay their quota, and all other like places also." The legislature agreed, and Montana dance halls were licensed for $400 a year.

That was not enough for Virginia City's residents, however. An irate subscriber wrote to the editor of the *Montana Post:* "Why don't you pitch into that infernal nuisance on Jackson Street, called by some a dance house? I live a few doors from it, and nearly every night my rest is broken by the shouts of drunken prostitutes and their partners. If the contemptible sum or license, which they pay, excuses their misdeeds, I and my unfortunate neighbors will agree to make up to the city what would be lost if the vile place was cleaned out."

Prostitutes, especially independents, usually made no pretense of selling anything but sex. These self-employed women occupied narrow shacks known as cribs, hotel rooms or houses of their own. Lillian Powers, "a nymph du prairie" who worked Cripple Creek, Colorado, in the 1890s, was a particularly successful exception to the general callousness that prevailed in the cribs. "I made good right away," Miss Lil reminisced to a historian. Contrary to the practice of her neighbors, who ran men in and out of unkempt shanties as fast as they could, Lil always kept her place neat and attractive, with clean linens and frilly curtains for the windows. Her regular customers could sit with her, enjoy a beer—at a price—and pour their troubles out to Lil's ever-sympathetic ear. By her own account, she developed a loyal clientele and made more profits in tips and beer than anyone else on the block made with sex as the only commodity.

However, professional rivalry soon forced Lil to leave Cripple Creek. She departed before dawn one morning, run out of town at gunpoint by Leo-the-Lion, a fading prostitute whose favorite customer had begun to see Lil on the sly. Lil repaired to Salida, Colorado, where she managed a local madam's cribs for a percentage of the take. Later she used the experience acquired in Salida to open her own house in nearby Florence.

A successful madam, especially one who managed a classy sporting house in a substantial town, had to be both charming and a capable, ruthless businesswoman. The madam set the tone for her house, and the tone determined the quality of her customers. She had to be adept at public relations and the soul of discretion. To recruit and hold on to a staff that was volatile by nature, she had to be at once tough and motherly. There was always a rowdy customer to eject without a disturbance, a bar to look after and, in the fanciest places, a kitchen to supervise.

A madam's girls generally worked on commissions, splitting their fees evenly with the house. In Denver the charge was commonly five dollars for a "quick date" and up to $30 for the entire night. Any tips belonged to the employee. In some houses, to keep the madam and the girls from cheating each other, the customer purchased a "brass check," a metal token passed to the prostitute in exchange for her services; the girls kept the tokens and settled up with the madam the next morning. The girls might also receive a cut on the drinks they promoted downstairs.

From their earnings the girls had to pay the madam rent for their rooms, ranging upward from about five dollars a week. And they were expected to dress themselves fashionably. A madam sometimes encouraged her prostitutes to charge clothing to her account with a dressmaker, thus securing a girl's loyalty through debt. Kickbacks to madams from dressmakers were com-

mon. For her part, the madam paid the expenses of running the house—salaries for domestics, bouncers, the piano player and a kitchen staff, payoffs to the police and fees for licenses. Despite heavy expenses, the madams—not the girls—were the ones who prospered. Yet few were able to preserve their wealth.

Jennie Rogers was an exception. She arrived in Denver late in 1879, flush with the proceeds from selling her bawdyhouse in St. Louis. Jennie had been set up in her Missouri establishment by the mayor of Pittsburgh after she had scandalized that city by serving as his honor's live-in housekeeper. Still earlier she had deserted her life as Leah Fries, a doctor's wife, to run away with Captain Rogers, a steamboat master from whom she took her professional name. By 1880, when she paid $4,600 for the house on Holladay Street, Denver, 36-year-old Jennie was already an established citizen of the sporting world.

Jennie had a weakness for spirited horses and reckless riding. In St. Louis she advertised her establishment by driving her finely attired courtesans about in a coach drawn by four horses. Within a year of her arrival in Denver she was arrested for "unladylike conduct in the street" after she and Eva Lewis, a friendly competitor, rode pell-mell on horseback through the city.

Except for the showy equestrienne in her, however, Jennie was extremely discreet. During the trial of a blackmailer in 1882, it became known that Jennie had paid him to keep her name out of the *Police Gazette* (at least one other Holladay Street madam had paid to get her name *into* the same paper). Jennie wanted no lurid publicity; she operated a classy house. In the *Denver Red Book: A Reliable Directory of the Pleasure Resorts of Denver,* published in 1892 after Holladay Street had been renamed Market Street, Jennie's advertisement was discreetly entered in the name of her bookkeeper. It read simply: "Ella Wellington, 1942 Market, Everything First-Class."

Jennie's flair for elegance drew Denver's best customers in droves, and by 1884 she was cramped in her original quarters. In the first of many expansions, Jennie built a three-story house with three parlors, a ballroom and a dining room to entertain gentlemen downstairs, and 15 bedrooms to entertain them upstairs. The biggest and best of her houses opened in 1889. The new house was promptly dubbed the Hall of Mirrors, for a

reflective parlor off the foyer. Now at her most popular, Jennie ran several sporting houses at once. She purchased the finest clothes, brought by shopkeepers to the brothel for her selection, and she entertained powerful and influential men.

During the 1880s and the early 1890s, the Colorado legislature's meeting place in Denver was only a short walk from the Hall of Mirrors. David Mechling, whose drugstore was located just a block away from Jennie's place, described the activity there while the legislature was in session: "Each afternoon about three o'clock the august lawmakers would retire to Jennie Rogers' on Market Street and there disport themselves in riotous fashion. Nothing was thought of that sort of thing in those days. It was a day of hard living. Men took their liquor neat and women took what they could get their hands on."

Jennie certainly lived up to Mechling's generalization about women. The way she hustled up the $17,780 required to construct her Hall of Mirrors, for instance, was distinctly illegal. Her lover in 1888 was a St. Louis police officer who discovered a dead-and-

buried scandal involving a man who had since become a prominent Denver banker. Armed with this information from her policeman, Jennie blackmailed the banker for $17,000. When it turned out months later that the estimate for building her house had been a trifle low, Jennie returned to her pigeon for an additional $780.

While still seeing the policeman, Jennie fell in love with Jack Wood, a 23-year-old hack driver. She took him out of his coach seat and established him in a saloon in Salt Lake City, far enough away from Denver so that Jack would not cross paths with Jennie's lawman. Although Jennie did not see anything wrong in having two men in her life, she drew the line at permitting Jack a similar privilege. When she surprised him in Utah with another woman in his arms, she staged a commotion that culminated in her shooting him. He survived and married her in August 1889. Jennie cherished the union. When Jack died only seven years later she erected a monument to him eight feet high; in 1909 when Jennie herself died, she was buried next to her husband. Her headstone reads: "Leah J. Wood," the name she had taken as Jack's wife. ◉

HAND-PAINTED DRESSING SCREEN

Gaudy opulence in bawdy Cripple Creek

ONE OF PEARL'S GIRLS

The Old Homestead reflected the instant excesses of a booming gold town. Parisian wallpaper set off the Italian furniture, and a profusion of crystal chandeliers and plush crimson velvet dazzled the eye. In the parlor, lamps glowed red beneath portraits of alluring young women. Upstairs, the bedrooms were furnished with velvet perfume boxes and screens for discreet dressing.

VELVET PERFUME BOX

In 1893, Pearl de Vere, a beautiful and enterprising young madam, moved her "parlor house" from Denver to Cripple Creek, Colorado, once it was known that money abounded there. A gold boom had turned the Rocky Mountain backwater into a high-living mining camp; when Miss Pearl arrived, swarms of prospectors were reaping hundreds of thousands of dollars a month and spending it just as fast.

Miss Pearl set up shop in a modest house on Myers Avenue. She was so successful that when fire demolished the town three years later, she was back in business within weeks in a much more grandiose establishment eventually filled with the ornate furnishings shown here. Her new, two-story, pink brick house in the heart of the red-light district was called the Old Homestead and its fame soon spread the 100 miles to Denver, and beyond.

The Old Homestead was elegant, exclusive and expensive. To get past the starched maid at the front door, one needed not only a thick wallet—a visit cost $50 to $100—but also a formal letter of introduction. Yet the guests paid gladly to taste the fine food, drink the free-flowing champagne, listen to music provided by a piano player and enjoy the company of auburn-haired Pearl and her gifted "boarders."

PARLOR LAMP

ITALIAN FRUIT
COMPOTE

CHINA SPITTOON

HAND-CARVED LIQUOR CABINET

In addition to its lavish decorations, the Old Homestead boasted the most up-to-date amenities. Many of the guests were exposed for the first time to recorded music and electricity. Two bathrooms with running water were a special luxury, and a domestic staff of seven kept the liquor chest and fruit dishes full and the spittoons empty. Miss Pearl's girls sat clutching the back of the chair shown below as they were laced into their corsets and took belladonna to relieve the resulting pain. Pearl herself died in 1897 from an overdose of the painkiller morphine.

EDISON STANDARD
PHONOGRAPH

BELLADONNA
LEAVES IN CANNISTER

WASH BASIN AND
PITCHER

EARTHENWARE
FOOT WARMER

CORSET CHAIR

Long standing revulsion toward women in medicine still flourished in 19th Century America. "We hope never to see the day," declared a medical journal of 1867, "when female character shall be so completely unsexed, as to fit it for the disgusting duties which imperatively devolve upon one who would attain proficiency, or even respectability, in the healing art." In other words, doctoring was man's work, too nasty and too intimate for the delicate sensibilities of true womanhood. Even if a woman was thick-skinned, resourceful and persistent enough to earn a degree, people still doubted her capabilities. A woman doctor, even more than a man, had to prove herself, and after she did, most of her practice was confined to women patients.

Beginning in the 1870s, a fair number of women entered the medical arena in the West. In 1870 Dr. Sarah Hall, who specialized in treating women's and children's diseases, began practice in Fort Scott, Kansas. A few years later in San Francisco, Dr. Charlotte Brown began an innovative medical career that included the founding in that city of the Pacific Dispensary for Women and Children. In 1873 Mary Sawtelle became the first woman to graduate with a medical degree from Willamette University in Salem, Oregon. And that same year, Bethenia Owens left Roseburg, Oregon, for Philadelphia to begin a career in medicine that typified the pioneer professional woman who had the courage to challenge the repressive social conventions of her generation.

Bethenia Owens—who hyphenated her name to Owens-Adair after marrying her second husband, John Adair—led a varied and hectic life on the circuitous way to becoming a doctor. One of nine children of parents who had been among Oregon's first settlers, Dr. Owens recalled that "I was the family nurse; and it was seldom that I had not a child in my arms."

Her life away from home began conventionally enough when she married Legrand Hill at 14—not an unusual age on the early frontier—then bore a son two years later. By the time her marriage foundered in 1859, Bethenia had acquired a fiercely independent spirit. Refusing to accept charity even from her family, she earned money to pay relatives and friends for her room and board by taking in washing, ironing and sewing, by berrypicking and also by nursing.

Getting an education was not easy. Bethenia literally had to work as she studied; when a friend called on her one evening, he found her ironing and reading at the same time. But she learned enough to begin teaching in 1861, gaining a steadier source of income that assured her complete independence. Bethenia saved most of her wages as a teacher and when she had accumulated $400, she purchased a lot and "contracted with a carpenter to build a small, three-room cottage, with a cozy little porch" in Astoria, Oregon.

At about this time, Legrand Hill, Bethenia's former husband, turned up on her doorstep. He had written to her often, beseeching her to remarry him, but Bethenia had always declined, politely but firmly. Now he stood before her, hoping that his presence would overcome her opposition. "But alas for him," wrote Bethenia. "He found not the young, ignorant, inexperienced child-mother whom he had neglected and misused, but a full-grown, self-reliant woman who could look upon him only with pity."

Partly at her parents' urging, Bethenia returned to Roseburg, where she opened a dress and millinery shop. For two years, Bethenia prospered unchallenged in her new endeavor. Then came the first acrid taste of competition; a new milliner, more experienced and skillful than Bethenia, moved into town.

As Bethenia recalled, "All this was not only humiliating to me personally, but was a severe blow to my business." But one sunny day, Bethenia's nemesis moved her workroom outside, where she could be seen from Bethenia's window. "For more than an hour I sat there," Bethenia wrote, "and in that brief time I learned the art of cleaning, stiffening, fitting, bleaching, and pressing hats," skills she had never known before. In this way, she began to revitalize her business. Then to upstage her competition even more, she traveled to San Francisco for instruction from professional milliners. Armed with her new knowledge, Bethenia was able to earn a $1,500 profit in the first year after she arrived back in Roseburg.

When at last her son, George, was at college in California and the difficult times were behind her, Bethenia might have slipped into complacency. Instead, she decided to embark on still another new course that would propel her into a maelstrom of controversy: Bethenia Owens would become Dr. Owens.

Dr. Bethenia Owens, still a milliner in this picture, once had to prove that she was indeed a physician before incredulous American customs agents passed her medical instruments into the country duty-free.

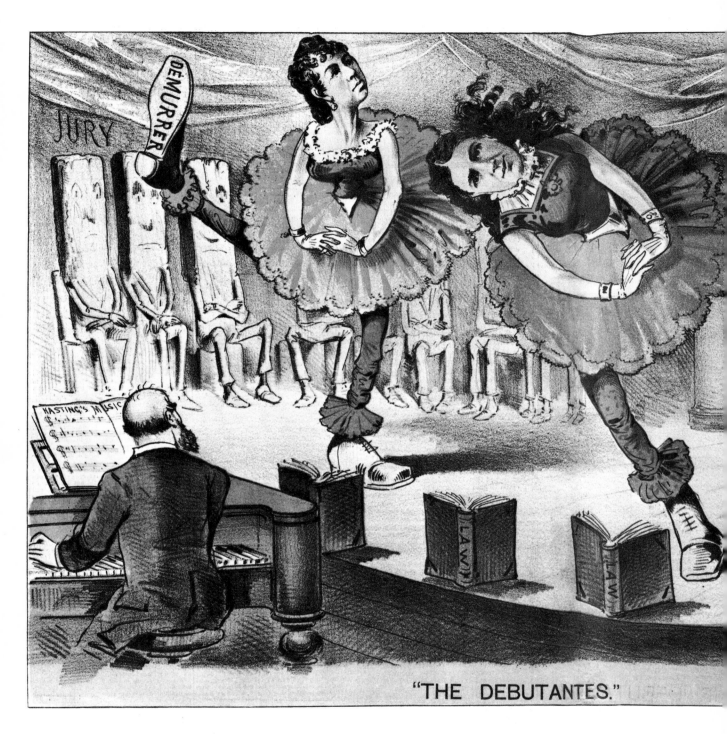

"THE DEBUTANTES."

her success with the legislature. But on the second day she appeared for class, her way was barred by a janitor who had instructions to keep her from entering. The janitor relented when Clara reappeared with a note from Judge Hastings, founder of the law school, that would allow her to be admitted until the school's board of directors could decide whether women could attend. The following day, the board decided against Clara on the ground that it had the right to refuse admission to those whose presence would be "useless to such persons themselves, or detrimental to said college, or likely to impair or interfere with the proper discipline and instruction of the students."

The students, indeed, had behaved like spoiled children during Clara's brief sojourn in their midst. "The first day," she recalled, "I had a bad cold and was forced to cough. To my astonishment every young man in the class was seized with a violent fit of coughing. If I

district court Clara argued that Hastings was a part of the University of California system and, as such, could not deny her admission because of her sex. The college argued that by virtue of the private grant that established it, Hastings was not part of the university system and could exclude whom it pleased. Clara presented her case "with both force and polish," according to one newspaper report. On the other hand, the opposing attorney—a former U.S. district attorney for California named Delos Lake—strayed into the usual homilies about women's proper sphere and warned that "lady lawyers were dangerous to justice inasmuch as an impartial jury would be impossible when a lovely woman pleaded the case of the criminal."

Clara sniffed victory: "I closed my argument conscious that I had won my case." And the judge agreed. His ruling in her favor was later sustained in the state supreme court and she resumed classes late in 1879.

Ironically, Clara never received her degree; the pressure of a successful practice forced her to give up her studies after two years. Laura Gordon, however, passed her bar examination without returning to Hastings College, hung out her shingle in San Francisco and eventually was admitted to practice before the United States Supreme Court.

Clara Foltz's early years as a lawyer earned her a reputation as a compassionate and understanding counselor, and she attracted many clients who could not pay for her services. "I kept myself continually impoverished by what my friends declared was unwise generosity," she recalled. But her dealings with indigents stimulated her interest in reforming the California criminal justice system—she pushed through legislation for a public-defender operation that became the model for other states—and brought to her an increasingly remunerative criminal practice.

Clara Foltz's broad interests led her into politics, into business, where she made profitable investments, and into publishing. Looking back on her life in anticipation of an autobiography that she never completed, Mrs. Foltz wrote: "Everything in retrospect seems weird, phantasmal, and unreal. I peer back across the misty years into that era of prejudice and limitation, when a woman lawyer was a joke, but the story of my triumphs will eventually disclose that though the battle has been long and hard-fought, it was worth while."

turned over a leaf in my note book every student in class did likewise. If I moved my chair—hitch went every chair in the room. I don't know what ever became of the members of that class. They must have been an inferior lot, for certain it is, I have never seen nor heard tell of one of them from that day to this."

Clara, once again on the outside looking in, joined with Laura Gordon, another aspiring law student, in a suit to force Hastings College to let them attend. In

Oregon women, proud of family businesses they helped make successful, boost their enterprises with signs and banners made for an 1890s parade. The skull and crossbones in the center advertises a pharmacy.

EUGENE
MILLS
EUGENE
MILL & ELEVATOR CO.
SPRRCo
RAATHS AND HOUSER
BLACK SMITH'S
OAKLAND
BUILDING
BRASS
BAND

5 | A burst of free spirits

"Proper women"—ladies who conformed to the conventional roles as wives and mothers—were horrified and angered by the flamboyant doings of Martha Jane Cannary, who won deathless notoriety as Calamity Jane. During the 1870s gold rush in Dakota Territory, when she worked briefly as a bartender in Deadwood, Calamity Jane had to act fast to save herself from "the good virtuous women" of the community, who, she said, "planned to run me out of town. They came into the saloon with a horse whip and shears to cut off my hair. I jumped off the bar into their midst and before they could say sickem I had them bowling."

Such accounts contributed to Calamity Jane's reputation as a woman who did what she pleased. A penchant for lying helped, too. She claimed, unsupportably, to have been an Army scout, a wagon freighter and an Indian fighter. All that is known for sure is that she was a brawling alcoholic who sometimes worked as a prostitute.

Fortunately for the peace and morals of the frontier, most independent female spirits in the West—and there were many—expressed their individualism in less violent and distasteful ways than did Calamity Jane. They, too, braved opprobrium to challenge the conventions that limited their activities as women. Although most went about this quietly, they were as stubborn as was Calamity in insisting on living as they wished. And in doing so, they helped win new freedom and greater opportunities for all women.

An aging nonconformist, Calamity Jane visits the Deadwood grave of Wild Bill Hickok around 1900. Claiming to be Bill's widow, Calamity wanted to be buried beside him and, in 1903, she was.

159

Defiant women who lived as they pleased

For a time it seemed that the West was the perfect place for a woman to express herself—to articulate the private feelings and aspirations she had so long suppressed. Indeed, most of the stories women heard in the East characterized the frontier settlements as informal, cooperative, tolerant and marvelously free. Westerners were widely and justly celebrated as rugged individualists, which suggested they would not deny any newcomers—even women—the cherished privilege of being left alone and, within reason, doing as they pleased.

As a result, the West attracted a legion of nonconforming women: mavericks, loners, eccentrics, adventurers. Some of these free spirits defied the traditional notion of a woman's place and a woman's work in small ways: riding astride and suiting their own tastes in attire. More radical women competed for jobs ordinarily filled by men. And then there were a few who were not only unconventional but also lamentably antisocial; they embraced the dangerous and usually unprofitable career of the Western outlaw.

But the West was no woman's oyster, whether she was law-abiding or otherwise. Once a frontier community was solidly established, the stultifying social conventions of the East came pouring in. Prime among these shibboleths was the firm conviction among males—and a great many females—that home was the only proper place for a woman and that her only proper work was caring for her husband and children. It is important to note that most women agreed with this belief, and the fact that most of them conformed to it made life harder for those who would not.

The question of whether the West was truly a freer place for women was widely argued. One who decided it was not was Mary Hallock Foote, a respected chronicler of family life in California and Colorado (pages 104-105). As much as Mrs. Foote deplored the "perpetuated grooves and deep-rooted complexities" of life in her native state of New York, she asserted that mature Eastern towns were "freer and more cheerful" than the raw Western communities. "No society," she concluded, "is so puzzling in its relations, so exacting in its demands upon self-restraint, as one which has no methods, which is yet in the state of fermentation."

But many women of independent mind, high spirit and strong ambition found the fermenting West less rigid and thus more susceptible to change than the East. Any woman who dared to venture out on an uncharted course stood a better chance in the West of reaching her objective—even if she did have to endure what one early comer described as society's reaction to nonconformists: "unkind feeling, even without supposing bitter animosity."

These defiant spirits paid a price for marching to a different drummer. They suffered snubs and censure and were the subject of idle or malicious gossip. Most of them simply shrugged it off. A few positively relished the scandals they caused.

Among these last was Lillie Hitchcock Coit. Lillie's father was a physician who, despite considerable inherited wealth, chose to work as an Army doctor. He was transferred from Atlanta to San Francisco in the spring of 1851 when Lillie was seven years old. Two days before Christmas she was plucked unharmed from an upper floor of a blazing hotel by a burly fireman from Knickerbocker Number Five, one of the many volunteer fire companies of which pioneer San Franciscans were justly proud. The dramatic rescue made an indelible impression on Lillie, and before long she was a

---

Carefree Kitty Tatch cavorts with a friend high above Yosemite Valley in 1900. Kitty autographed postcards of her antics at a nearby hotel where she was a waitress.

familiar figure at fires, cheering her hero firemen on. Soon she was Number Five's unofficial mascot, and by the end of the decade this sparkling-eyed little girl had become a fixture in the parades and celebrations of all the city's fire companies.

Lillie was no great beauty, but as a symbol of the all-important volunteer fire fighters she was widely recognized as a fresh young symbol of the rapidly growing city itself. And she was more than just a mascot—intelligent and quick-witted, she was an accomplished singer, dancer and guitarist. By her 18th birthday, Lillie was the undisputed belle of San Francisco. She was also rich in her own right, having inherited property and $60,000 in cash from her grandfather. And though she barely knew him, she had fallen in love with

the wealthy and handsome young Howard Coit, son of a prominent surgeon, and had made up her mind to marry him some day.

With her mother, a Southern sympathizer, Lillie spent part of the Civil War years in Europe. She kept the home folks posted with occasional newspaper dispatches that included such witticisms as, "The two most precious things to men come in hoops: girls and whiskey." Returning to California before the end of the War, Lillie discovered that she was considered, as a newspaper had said during her absence, "San Francisco's brightest ornament."

Among other tributes, she was given a certificate of membership in her beloved Knickerbocker Number Five, making her the only woman in the United States to belong to a volunteer fire company. It was said that from then on she observed this status by having the numeral 5 embroidered on her undergarments. Lillie's casual attitude toward courtship had earned her a reputation as a coquette; once she was engaged to two men and wore their rings on alternate days. But though scores of suitors sought her hand, she stuck to her prewar resolve to marry Howard Coit.

Coit could have had his choice of San Francisco's beauties, but he was enchanted by the high-spirited Lillie Hitchcock, who continued to defy convention by engaging in such unladylike pastimes as poker playing and betting on horses. The two were married in 1868, and they threw themselves headlong into San Francisco's social swirl.

It was soon apparent, however, that Howard had a roving eye that had not been stilled by his wedding vows. Lillie tried to keep her straying husband occupied with such whirlwind escapades as disguising herself as a man and going along with him to watch a cockfight. But nothing helped. The unhappy situation dragged on until the early 1880s, when Lillie decided to leave Coit and live in a country place built for her by her doting father.

For a time, Lillie practically withdrew from San Francisco society. But in 1885 Howard Coit died of a heart ailment at the age of 47, leaving Lillie a $250,000 estate. Perhaps he had loved her after all. In any case, he doubtless would have approved when, before long, Lillie resumed a frantic round of eccentric activity. For starters, she went on an overnight camping trip with five men. Not long afterward she disguised herself as a portly, black-bearded man and went roistering through the lowest dives on the waterfront with four male admirers. "There isn't another woman in all San Francisco as unladylike as you," an acquaintance rebuked her. "Shush!" said Lillie. "You must be forgetting yourself."

On one memorable occasion, eager to see one of the prize fights that so intrigued her male friends, she had a pair of professional boxers brought to her suite in the elegant Palace Hotel. Furniture and bric-a-brac were cleared from the parlor; the two pugilists stripped for action and began slugging away. After a few rounds the referee turned to Lillie, who was ensconced in a plush chair atop a table, and asked if the fight should be declared a draw. Like a Roman empress of old, Lillie gave the thumbs-down sign and forced the match to its conclusion, a bloody knockout.

The parlor fisticuffs made news across the country. The *Boston Globe* hailed Lillie for pioneering a new way of life for women. But the *New York World* professed indignation; the affair was "a staggering shock," the paper said, adding sarcastically that "it did not ruffle San Francisco one bit. They are used to her."

Perhaps so, but even San Francisco was fast outgrowing the no-holds-barred world of Lillie Coit. At the turn of the century a new scandal erupted when a distant relative of Lillie's, enraged that he had not been chosen to manage her financial affairs, came after her with a gun; another man was killed trying to protect her. By now the city had had enough of its erstwhile ornament. "Lillie Hitchcock Coit was once the idol of San Francisco," one newspaper intoned. "Now the city is too big and too old to have such idols."

Soon after that Lillie fled the city, and she spent most of the rest of her life abroad. But memories mellowed with time, and she returned at last. When she died at 85 she bequeathed $100,000 to San Francisco. Recalling the days when a sprightly, bright-eyed girl had been a mascot for the Knickerbocker Number Five, the city used the bequest to raise a monument to fire fighters in Washington Square and to build an observation tower, named in Lillie's honor, on top of Telegraph Hill.

Lillie Coit had plenty of money, which always has enhanced an eccentric's chances of being popularly accepted. But at roughly the same time, in Montana, another female free spirit was also becoming a legend by defiantly insisting on being herself, and she did so without any of Lillie Coit's worldly advantages. In fact, Mary Fields had begun life in Tennessee with a distinct disadvantage: she was born a slave. Eschewing humility, this belligerently self-reliant woman—six feet tall and weighing 200 pounds, she allegedly could whip any man her size—compelled her chosen Western neighbors in Cascade, Montana, where she spent the last 30 years of her life, to accept her on her own unconventional terms.

"Black Mary," as she was known, was a living monument to the radical idea that a woman could do anything a man could do. She regularly toted guns and sometimes used them. She became the second woman in history to work as a driver of a United States mail coach and the first woman in Cascade to be officially granted the privilege of drinking in the town's saloons, normally off-limits to females. Not only did her neighbors eventually accept her way of life, they came to revere her for it. In her later years Cascade's public schools closed in honor of Mary's birthday, sometimes—because she was uncertain of the date and enjoyed celebrations—twice a year.

Mary Fields, who had been fighting for her rights and her daily bread all her life, was already past 50 when she moved to Cascade in 1884 and was hired by St. Peter's, a Catholic mission about 20 miles outside of town. Her job, which she held for the next eight years, consisted of hauling freight and helping out with heavy chores. With a fat cigar clamped in her jaw and a jug of whiskey at her side, and usually armed with both a rifle and a revolver, she at first presented a less-than-respectable image to the townsfolk. Schoolchildren looked in awe on the "bad woman" as she drove her wagon to meet the trains.

Mary ignored the stares and got on with her work, which sometimes meant managing eight horses pulling two wagons in tandem. Her freight runs were risky as well as arduous. As she hurried back to the mission one night, wolves attacked her wagon and the horses bolted, spilling Mary and all of her supplies onto the ground. She spent the next several hours fending off the varmints with her guns.

Mary was not an unfriendly woman, but anyone who incurred her wrath would have made a dangerous enemy. Once when a hired hand at St. Peter's insulted her, she would be satisfied with nothing less than a showdown with guns. The man's shots went wild and Mary aimed just close enough to frighten him and drive him away. The shoot-out did no damage—except to the patience of the Bishop of Helena, who was inundated with complaints about "that black woman." He gave Mary the sack.

Mary moved into town and opened a little restaurant. After a while she went broke; she had gone hungry too often herself to deny a free meal to any penniless traveler. But by now her neighbors were being won over by her bigheartedness and indepen-

Where ladies were liberated

American men who traveled the Santa Fe Trail in the early 1800s met women in New Mexico whose freedom of dress and action would not be equaled elsewhere in the West for almost a hundred years. For the Americans, it was a cultural shock, but fascinating.

Unencumbered by petticoats, bustles, corsets or long sleeves, Mexican women—said author Stanley Vestal—"never heard of underwear" and "wore a skimpy *camiso,* short red skirts, gay shawls, and slippers. They made what seemed a prodigal display of their charms." To newcomer Lewis Garrard, the low-cut dresses and displays of flesh were "uncomely." Chronicler George Kendall, too, was at first shocked by the "Eve-like and scanty garments," but eventually declared them preferable to American dress.

Kendall was also won over by the uninhibited nature of the women, whom he described as being "joyous, sociable, kind-hearted creatures, liberal to a fault, easy and naturally graceful in their manners."

Two women smoke *cigaritos* in a New Mexico doorway.

Irish-born Nellie Cashman became the philanthropic "angel" of a dozen rough mining towns. Oddly, this portrait was painted in China from a photograph her Chinese cook took along on a visit home.

Arcade Restaurant & Chop House

Allen Street, Vizina Block, Tombstone, A. T.

Miss Nellie Cashman, Proprietress.

LATE OF THE DELMONICO, TUCSON.

Meals at All Hours.

Regular Dinner from 4 to 7 p. m. Open Until 8 p. m.!

dence — and by her celebrity, which grew as tales of her exploits circulated through the territory. When she was in her sixties, she was given a job driving the United States mail; she proved herself a swift courier who could not be stopped by flood or blizzard, and public admiration for her deeds mounted.

In her seventies, too old to keep driving, Mary operated a laundry in her home. As a gesture of respect, Cascade's Mayor D. W. Monroe gave her special permission to drink in the town's saloons, and, between washes, she joined the men in hoisting a glass — and then another. "She could drink more whiskey than anyone I ever knew," recalled one Cascade male. Mary's exuberance began to fade before her time ran out in 1914. But on appropriate occasions her old proud belligerence broke through again, as it did one day when a customer who had neglected to pay his laundry bill happened to pass the saloon where she was drinking. Mary spotted him, stepped outside, knocked the man flat with one punch, then contentedly rejoined her companions. That account, she announced, was now settled in full.

While Mary Fields's legendary status was pretty much restricted to Montana, another woman who lived exactly as she pleased was talked and written about all up and down the frontier. Nellie Cashman, one of the most famous Western women of her day, was one of the few nonconformists who won immediate and universal ac-

ceptance in spite of her unladylike career — prospecting. The reason for her popularity is evident in some of the appellations she earned during the 50 adventurous years that she trekked all over the West, from Alaska to Mexico, in quest of pay dirt. She was called the Frontier Angel, the Angel of Tombstone, the Miner's Angel and the Saint of the Sourdoughs. These admiring sobriquets were given to her because her thirst for adventure was coupled with a strong, merciful compassion that never let her pass by another human being in need of assistance.

Nellie loved to make money and was very good at it; several rich strikes and various mining-town businesses earned her half a dozen fortunes. However, everything she acquired she gave away to those less able to take care of themselves. She donated large sums to frontier hospitals and church missions, and she personally fed, housed, nursed and grubstaked innumerable hard-luck prospectors. Some of her friends concluded that Nellie made money just to support her true vocation: doing good. One of her many ardent admirers called her "the best woman I ever knew."

In acquiring her fortunes and her reputation, she frequently risked her life, and her bold and strenuous exploits conjured up a picture of a muscular and grim-faced Amazon, somewhat like "Black Mary" Fields. But in actual fact Nellie was just a little over five feet tall and slender, with delicate feminine features and lustrous dark eyes. Her nephew, Michael Cunning-

On June 20, 1890, Elizabeth Potts *(above)* and her husband, Josiah, were hanged in Elko, Nevada, for murdering Miles Faucett. His mutilated body had been found buried in their cellar. To the end, the Pottses staunchly claimed their innocence. Only after their execution was a motive for the murder discovered: Elizabeth had bigamously married Faucett in California, then tired of him and rejoined her legal husband in Nevada. Faucett had followed her and probably threatened to expose her unless she returned to him. The town of Elko imported a gallows *(right)* from California and sent out printed invitations to the double hanging. Mrs. Potts climbed the gallows wearing a white muslin suit with a red rose pinned to her bodice.

A few women went much further than Nellie Cashman in discarding traditionally feminine ways. These women denied their sex completely and disguised themselves as men. This was, to say the least, a radical step, and they did not take it just for a lark, or even as a challenge to prove their abilities in competition with men. Rather, they felt that their opportunities as women were severely limited by society's restraints and that there was no other way for them to live the untrammeled life they longed for or to do satisfying work or simply to get a tolerable, well-paying job. Obviously, however, a life in disguise had severe limitations of its own. To keep her secret, the masquerader was obliged to be a loner, to have no close friends of either sex, to go about her business as guardedly as a fugitive from justice, always fearing her true identity would somehow be discovered.

In spite of these drawbacks, an ersatz male known as Charley Parkhurst apparently enjoyed a happy life and realized all her ambitions while passing as a man. The sketchy accounts of her life indicate that she was born Charlotte Parkhurst or Pankhurst in New Hampshire around 1812 and that she first donned male attire in order to make good her escape from an orphanage. She may never have presented herself as a female again.

Charley served an apprenticeship in various menial jobs in New England, all of them involving work with horses. She was small but wiry and strong, and had a gift for handling animals; she lived with them in the stables to preserve her secret but claimed she did so because she got on better with horses than with people.

When gold was discovered at Sutter's Mill, Charley followed the great rush to California. There she became a crack stagecoach driver, famed for whipping her teams at a fast pace down narrow, plunging mountain trails. Though she was a familiar character in the mining camps, her disguise remained undetected until her death in 1879. Then the world learned of her secret through an article in the San Francisco *Chronicle*.

Ironically, later Californians honored Charley Parkhurst not for excelling at man's work but for simply being a member of the sex she had disowned. A bronze plaque erected in the town of Soquel, where the duly-registered Charley Parkhurst had voted in November 1868, proclaimed that it marked the site where the first woman cast a ballot in a Presidential election.

If, as seems likely, Charley Parkhurst never felt regret for her lost womanhood, her feelings were far different from those of Elsa Jane Forest Guerin, who spent 13 years disguised as a man, five of them adventuring in the early West. After her true identity was revealed in 1859, she wrote a memoir that, though patently a melodramatic potboiler, revealed her masquerade as a deeply disturbing experience.

Elsa Jane wrote that she was the illegitimate offspring of a well-to-do Louisiana planter and an overseer's wife. Her father, a bachelor, sheltered her in his mansion as his niece until he judged her old enough to be packed off to boarding school. There, she said, "I developed with a rapidity marvelous even in that hotbed, the South," and at the implausible age of 12 she ran off to St. Louis with the first young man to pay her court. His name was Forest and he was, she learned after their marriage, a pilot on a Mississippi riverboat.

Elsa Jane bore Forest two children, and for four years she was a happy housewife. Then one day a messenger came bearing the news that her husband had been killed in a fight with a member of his crew, a man named Jamieson. The sudden tragic loss nearly crushed Elsa Jane, as it might have any 16-year-old. Her husband had left no savings; she was destitute and alone.

How was the young widow to earn a living? She had never learned a trade and, she said, "I knew how great are the prejudices to be overcome by any young woman who seeks to earn an honest livelihood by her own exertions." Thus she devised a scheme of disguising herself as a man to apply for a man's job. The disguise would serve a dual purpose: it would also help her find and punish her husband's killer, who was now a free man. Jamieson had been convicted for the killing, but the verdict had been overturned on a technicality.

Her "soul filled with poignant grief" at the parting, Elsa Jane put her children in the care of the Sisters of Charity. Assuming her male disguise—which included a conscious effort to use rough language and to speak in a gravelly voice—she began looking for work. She was greeted with rebuffs and casual rudeness, but the rough treatment was beneficial, stiffening her resolve. "I buried my sex in my heart," she wrote, "and roughened the surface so that the grave would not be discovered."

At last Elsa Jane was offered a job: $35 a month to serve as cabin boy on a steamer plying between St.

The ghastly harvest of Katie Bender's garden

For two years, beginning in 1872, a succession of travelers disappeared from the area around Cherryvale, on the lonely plains of southeastern Kansas. The uncovering of their fate revealed a tale of horror that rivaled the grimmest of gothic novels.

For a long time no one suspected the Benders, a family of German immigrants who had bought two tracts of land and built a one-room frame house, where they sold groceries and offered bed and board to wayfarers. Yet the Benders had some unsettling traits. Katie—the brains of the household and a great beauty—fancied herself a medium and sent out cards (right) claiming that she could cure the deaf and blind. Her father, a man of awesome strength, was sullen and brutish—as was his wife. Katie's brother, John Bender Jr., had a distracting habit of ending every remark with an idiotic laugh.

Despite reports from visitors who noticed bloodstains in the cabin or saw Pa Bender hefting a sledge hammer behind a curtain, no one questioned the family until a local physician disappeared. His brother, a prominent Kansas politician, went searching for him with a posse, and the trail led to the Benders.

Katie admitted that the doctor had been there, but said he had left after watering his horse. The posse was unsatisfied with her story and vowed to return. When they did, they found eight corpses, including that of the doctor, buried in the vegetable garden (below). The skulls had been bashed in and the throats slit, as in a ritual sacrifice. But Katie Bender and her family had vanished without a trace.

Prof. Miss KATIE BENDER

Can heal all sorts of Diseases; can cure Blindness, Fits, Deafness and all such diseases, also Deaf and Dumbness.

Residence, 14 miles East of Independence, on the road from Independence to Osage Mission one and one half miles South East of Norahead Station.

KATIE BENDER.

June 18, 1872.

Katie Bender distributed this card to local residents, promising to cure the incurable.

The curious came from miles to gawk at the graves of the Benders' victims and to pull slats from the house (at rear) for souvenirs.

Louis and New Orleans. For nearly four years she worked the river, advancing to second waiter. Once each month she changed into women's garb and visited her children. She even thought periodically of resuming her female role, but each time she was defeated by the problem of how she would continue to pay for the care and education of the children. Besides, "I began to rather like the freedom of my new character. I could go where I chose, do many things which while innocent in themselves, were debarred by propriety from association with the female sex. The change from the cumbersome, unhealthy attire of woman to the more convenient, healthful habiliments of man, was in itself almost sufficient to compensate for its unwomanly character."

In the spring of 1854, Elsa Jane was beached by a change of command on her riverboat. She found work as a brakeman on the Illinois Central Railroad. The new job went well until the conductor on her route made it clear, in a conversation that she happened to overhear, that he had seen through her disguise. She fled, ending her railroad career after eight months.

By then Elsa Jane was a captive of her masquerade. She confessed that even when she was at home in St. Louis, wearing women's clothes and visiting happily with her children, she could not shake off her studiously acquired masculine ways. On many a night she would surreptitiously don men's clothing and wander around town as free as the air—into the theater, onto the deck of a steamboat, in and out of hotel lobbies and smoke-filled saloons. Her conscience argued against these unnecessary rambles, yet she could not resist them.

On one such excursion, Elsa Jane spied Jamieson. And she was prepared, having purchased a revolver with which she intended to shoot him down "as I would a mad dog" whenever their paths might cross. Stealthily she trailed Jamieson through the streets. When he came to a lonely quarter of town, she challenged him. He also was armed, and they both fired.

Elsa Jane winged Jamieson but he ran away, avoiding the curiosity of the men who rushed up to see what had happened. Elsa Jane was wounded in the thigh and escaped detection only by dragging herself behind some shrubbery in a yard. The mistress of the house found her next morning and helped her inside. That lady, a widow herself, listened sympathetically to Elsa Jane's story and gave her refuge until she recovered.

In 1855 the storied riches of the West cast their spell over Elsa Jane. Once again in disguise, she joined a 60-man expedition to California. But her hopes of striking it rich in gold country quickly went aglimmering. By the time she arrived, the winter rains had begun, prices were sky-high and, worst of all, "I did not find my strength sufficient for the business" of prospecting.

Elsa Jane looked for more suitable work in Sacramento. Her best offer was a cleaning job in a saloon; it was dirty work, but Elsa Jane conceded that the $100-a-month salary was "somewhat of an offset against the peculiarities of the position." She lived frugally, saved her pay and after six months was able to buy a partnership in the saloon. Eight months later she sold out and began trading in pack mules. This venture proved so profitable that she went into freighting herself, shipping goods by mule train to the gold camps in the mountains.

As soon as she could arrange her thriving affairs, Elsa Jane sailed home for another visit with her children. For her return to California in 1857, she chose the overland route and, so as "not to go back empty handed," organized a train of 15 men, 20 mules and horses, and a herd of cattle. Her journey was plagued by bad luck; 110 head of cattle died from drinking alkali water, and when the train was attacked by a party of Snake Indians, some of the men—including the phony one—became casualties.

In spite of her livestock losses she had enough animals left to afford a small ranch in California's Shasta Valley. But she soon decided to sell the ranch and also her mule-freight business, which her chief assistant had run efficiently during her absence. After the sale of both enterprises, she sent "about $30,000" to St. Louis and soon followed her money home.

Elsa Jane had promised herself when she first left for California that "if I met with ordinary success I could retire into more private life, resume my proper dress, and thereafter in company with my children enjoy life to the full extent that circumstances would permit." When she had the prize in her grasp, however, it had lost its charm. She candidly admitted that "after staying awhile in St. Louis, I grew tired of the inactivity of my life and determined to seek adventure in some new direction." Resuming a man's role, she put in a stint as a trader for the American Fur Company, acquiring pelts from the Indians on the North and South Platte

Accepting a challenge to "any woman," daredevil Eunice Winkless plunges some 35 feet on a trained horse into a pool in Pueblo, Colorado, on July 4, 1905. Eunice had to sue to collect her $100 prize.

A Colorado huntress who immortalized her prey

Of all the displays at the 1876 U.S. Centennial Exhibition in Philadelphia, none was more popular than one in the Kansas and Colorado Building entitled "Woman's Work." On a simulated Western landscape were many animals that had been shot and mounted in lifelike attitudes by Martha Maxwell, a naturalist, hunter, taxidermist and artist.

Martha Maxwell obviously possessed skills that were rare for any woman, even on the Western frontier. When she was only 10 and living in Wisconsin, she picked up a gun and fired her first shot—killing a rattlesnake poised to strike her four-year-old sister. Later, she became an expert markswoman. Martha married James Maxwell and in 1860 moved with him to Colorado, where he owned a lumbermill.

Mrs. Maxwell was overwhelmed by Colorado's bounteous wildlife. After seeing the work of a local taxidermist, she decided to learn the art. Accompanying her husband on hunting trips in the Rockies, she carefully observed the actions of animals and birds in their natural habitats so that she could later create accurate reproductions. She reconstructed the animals' frames in plaster and stretched the treated skins over them.

At first, she displayed her specimens in her Boulder home. In 1873 the city offered her a hall, which she converted into the Rocky Mountain Museum—replete, as the *Boulder News* described it, with "every beast of the forest and plains, every bird of the air." Two years later she was persuaded to move the museum to Denver. There it came to the attention of state legislators, who invited her to show her works at the Centennial Exhibition.

Though Mrs. Maxwell was acclaimed as the only woman naturalist of her time, as well as the first taxidermist to place specimens in realistic poses and settings, she was sometimes criticized for shooting so many animals and birds. Her rejoinder: "There isn't a day you don't tacitly consent to have some creature killed so that you may eat it. I leave it to you. Which is more cruel? To kill to eat or to kill to immortalize?"

Mrs. Maxwell's specimens were not the only animals that brought her fame. In 1877 she was recognized as the discoverer of the Rocky Mountain screech owl, which was called *Scops Maxwelae* in her honor.

MRS. M. A. MAXWELL'S
Rocky Mountain Series,
COPY-RIGHT SECURED.

Martha Maxwell, known as "the Colorado Huntress," stands with her shotgun. Though she used the unusual method of sighting with her left eye, she was an expert shot who had no fear of camping alone in remote areas.

Dozens of stuffed animals stand in lifelike attitudes in Martha Maxwell's corner of the Centennial Exhibition. "I don't believe them critters was shot," stated one visitor. "I've looked 'em all over and I can't see any holes."

rivers, and was soon attracted to the Pikes Peak area where a major gold rush was in full swing. As in California, Elsa Jane had no luck at mining but again she did better in business. She opened an establishment in Denver called the Mountain Boy's Saloon and was known to her customers as "Mountain Charley."

The climax of Elsa Jane's masquerade came on an excursion outside Denver. As she was riding her mule alone through a narrow gorge, she saw a rider approaching from the opposite direction. Something about him looked familiar. At almost the same instant, she and Jamieson recognized each other.

Drawing one of her six-shooters, Elsa Jane tumbled her husband's killer from his saddle with her first shot as his bullet whizzed by her. Then, she admitted, "I emptied my revolver upon him as he lay, and should have done the same with its mate had not two hunters at that moment come upon the ground and prevented any further consummation of my designs." Still, her excitement had so unnerved her that she had failed to kill Jamieson, even at point-blank range. He actually recovered, and later left for New Orleans—only to die almost immediately of yellow fever.

Before Jamieson left Denver, however, he exposed Elsa Jane's camouflage and revealed as much of her personal history as he knew. He had also "exculpated me wholly from any blame in the attempts on his life." When the story got about, as it quickly did, Elsa Jane was famous. Though relieved that her life as a man had ended, she clung to her male attire. She did, however, get married again—to the bartender in her Denver saloon, who had known her first as Mountain Charley.

For all their success, the women who disguised themselves as men were avoiding, rather than challenging, the rigid conventions imposed upon their sex. The constructive nonconformists were the Nellie Cashmans and Mary Fieldses, who demanded acceptance on their own terms; they helped broaden the horizon for all Western women. More effective still were the persistent, defiant and sometimes intentionally obnoxious individualists whose achievements overshadowed their unpopularity and forced Westerners to question 19th Century notions of a woman's proper place.

One such woman appeared in Waller County, Texas, in 1873 and began searching for a place to live. She was Elisabet Ney, a striking red-haired virago of about 40. Except for her good looks, everything about her was offensive to the hard-scrabble farmers of the area.

Miss Ney spoke with a heavy German accent and claimed to be an artist. She wore outlandish getups: flowing Grecian gowns, or bloomers, or sometimes white trousers, a black frock coat and knee-high boots. Her entourage included a tall Scotsman, Dr. Edmund Duncan Montgomery, whom she referred to ambiguously as "my best friend," and two small boys, one of them an infant who was wheeled around in a fancy pram by a uniformed nurse, also a foreigner. When she found a run-down 1,100-acre plantation near the town of Hempstead, the exotic Miss Ney capped her local debut by flinging out her arms and crying theatrically, "Here will I live! And here will I die!"

At once the Texans began asking the natural questions. What was the relationship between this Ney person and the Scottish doctor? Were they married, and if so, why did she insist on being called Miss Ney? Or were they living in sin, and if so, were those two boys illegitimate? The community buzzed with gossip, but the newcomers were tolerated. This was Texas, after all, a wide-open country where interfering with other folks' business was not only rude but also dangerous: Hempstead, about 40 miles north of Houston, was such a rough town that it had earned the nickname "Six-Shooter Junction." In such a place you might not like your neighbors, but you did not crowd them.

The fact is that Elisabet Ney and the doctor were properly wed. But Elisabet considered marriage a form of slavery; she was so determined to keep her status a secret that she even made Edmund promise not to tell their own children. And she was indeed an artist—and not just an artist, but one who was famous in Europe. Among other commissions, she had on royal command sculpted the only bust ever made of Bismarck, the "Iron Chancellor" of Germany.

She and Montgomery had first met and fallen in love in 1852, while he was studying medicine at Heidelburg. Because of her philosophical opposition, they did not marry but led separate lives—he in London, she in Germany; they saw each other only when their work permitted. After 10 years Elisabet agreed to marry him—but only on Edmund's vow to keep the fact secret. For a while they lived in Madeira and then in Germany. In 1871 they accepted an invitation from one of Dr. Montgomery's former patients to join him in America and help found a back-to-nature colony of enlightened kindred spirits in Thomasville, Georgia. The agricultural colony was short-lived—its intellectual founders had no practical knowledge of farming—and soon the doctor and the artist were rootless again.

Miss Ney, who had stirred up even the progressive souls of the colony with the birth of her first (and apparently illegitimate) child, Arthur, traveled widely looking for a new home; she gave birth to her second child, Lorne, during the search. She finally chose southern Texas for its mild climate, which she thought would be good for her husband's health—he had suffered a bout of tuberculosis—and also for its large number of German families, who had been settling there since the 1830s.

At Liendo a curious living pattern soon evolved. Dr. Montgomery, who had a small inheritance, immersed himself in abstruse scientific research (he was seeking the answer to a question he posed in a scholarly paper entitled "To Be Alive—What Is It?"). Miss Ney did the work that normally fell to the head of a household. Determined to make the plantation support them, and in the process to help its black tenant families, she superintended the farming operations, kept the books, paid the bills. She was much too busy to pursue her art; when she had a little spare time, she spent it on horseback roaming the countryside, reveling in the sunshine, the clear air, the bluebonnets, the mockingbirds. Meanwhile, the nurse looked after the children.

Miss Ney had no interest in the affairs of the community and made no effort to cultivate its good will. She took pains, in fact, to show her disdain for the local ladies. One summer day a group of Hempstead women arrived at Liendo after a long journey to pay a courtesy call. The nurse seated them on folding stools in a crudely furnished parlor and went to get her mistress.

After a very long time the embarrassed nurse returned to say that Miss Ney could not see them because one of her sons was ill. The visitors expressed their sympathy and asked the nurse to tell Miss Ney that they, experienced mothers all, wished to help. The servant left the room again and returned with a firm rebuff: if Miss Ney needed their help, she would send a messenger to Hempstead to let them know. Such brusqueness was easily misconstrued as a sign of guilt—an effort to conceal, the locals imagined, the irregularities in her household.

The suspicious and resentful townspeople were driven almost beyond their natural Western reluctance to interfere some months later when tragedy struck at Liendo. The little boy called Arthur fell sick and died, but there was no public funeral service or burial. Soon the whole county was rife with stories about what that monstrous woman and the foreign doctor had done with the child's body. One rumor said that the sculptor had encased the little corpse in plaster and had stood the resulting statue on a hall table at Liendo. Another account said that she had stored the body in the plantation's cistern hoping the cold water would preserve it, and then, hearing that the county health officer was coming to investigate, took it out and secretly buried it by a creek. Still another whispered story alleged that the boy's remains had been burned up in Liendo's big fireplace. Cremation was at that time an abhorred practice. The town was shocked and outraged.

For two or three weeks after Arthur's death Hempstead trembled on the brink of violence. The Ku Klux Klan, powerful in the area, planned a punitive visit to Liendo. The Klansmen vowed to find the child's body—or his ashes—and give him a Christian burial. They were also going to force Miss Ney to promise that she would start wearing skirts instead of trousers. Moreover, they were determined to clear up the question of her relationship with Dr. Montgomery; the couple would have to produce a marriage license, the Klan proclaimed, or leave the county within 12 hours.

Isolated as Miss Ney and her husband were from the life of the community—and especially so now as they sought seclusion to grieve their small son's death—they apparently were not aware of the threatened Klan raid. Their Hempstead lawyers, Ab Lipscomb and Tom Reese, were very much aware of it, however, and worked diligently and loyally to head it off. Over a period of days the lawyers sought out the town's Klansmen one by one and told them the true story of what had happened at Liendo. Yes, the couple had burned up the boy's body—but with good reason. Arthur had died of diphtheria and his grief-stricken parents, acting with great personal courage, had cremated him to prevent the spread of the highly conta-

gious disease. They should be respected for protecting the public's health, the lawyers said, and be left to live their own lives as they wished. On learning the facts, Hempstead calmed down and the Klansmen put their sheets back in their linen cupboards.

Miss Ney was shattered by the death of her beloved "Arti." Before performing the dread task of cremation, she had made a death mask of him, which she kept in a trunk with her other personal treasures for the rest of her life. She became overzealous in the upbringing of her surviving son, Lorne. She dressed him in girlish-looking costumes, such as little Roman togas, and refused to let him play with the neighbors' sons, whom she considered hoodlums. She had him tutored at home—when she could find tutors.

Unfortunately for Lorne his mother did not seem to appreciate the difference between defying convention herself and compelling a small boy to do the same. Once when he was six, she offered to take him on a rare trip to Hempstead. Lorne, who thought nothing was more exciting than the town's railroad yard with its steam shunting engine puffing back and forth, was elated. Dressed in sandals, tunic and long white toga, the innocent child set off with his mother in a buggy.

Miss Ney left him in the vehicle while she did business in a Hempstead shop. When she emerged she found the buggy surrounded by a mob of town boys shouting "Come out, shirt tail! Come out!" There was no sign of Lorne. The taunting children dispersed as she approached and then she found her son—huddled under the buggy seat, sobbing and trying to hide the costume that had made him an object of ridicule. It is no wonder that when Lorne reached adolescence, he was in open rebellion against his mother, who for all he knew had borne him illegitimately. Though he was smart, he did poorly at a succession of prep schools and grew up to be an unstable, oft-married charmer.

Miss Ney was upset by her son's development, but not enough so to alter her own eccentric behavior. She continued her unladylike existence, spurning the locals and doing the man's job of overseeing the plantation. For years she strived in vain to make the place pay. Quixotically, she tried to solve the problem by enlarging the property; by 1887 she had acquired 1,200 additional acres that did nothing but put further strain on Dr. Montgomery's income. The plantation would probably have failed even if Miss Ney had known how to run it; there were no local markets for her crops and long-distance shipping was primitive and costly.

Having failed as an agricultural businesswoman, Miss Ney turned again to her art, and in this endeavor the same arrogance and highfalutin ideas that had offended her neighbors stood her in good stead. In 1872 Oren Milo Roberts, then a candidate for governor of Texas, had passed through Hempstead and visited Liendo. Roberts, who wanted to encourage the growth of culture in the state, was intrigued by the talented and strong-willed sculptor. Later, after being elected governor, he returned to Liendo and sat for a bust by Miss Ney, which won wide praise when displayed in Austin.

Roberts' sponsorship helped her win a momentous commission: to sculpt full-length statues of Texas heroes Sam Houston and Stephen F. Austin for the Chicago World's Columbian Exposition in 1893.

To carry out her commission, Miss Ney left Liendo in Dr. Montgomery's care, moved to Austin and built a studio, which she named Formosa after their honeymoon villa on Madeira. While the carpenters and masons worked, she camped in a tent on the grounds, the better to supervise every detail of the construction. Formosa, completed in 1891, was the first building erected in Texas solely for artistic purposes.

Now 59 years old, Miss Ney was soon at work with youthful vigor and enthusiasm. Her work was lavishly praised at the Columbian exposition. Afterward, the original statues were placed in the Texas state capitol and copies were made for permanent display in the national Capitol in Washington.

Miss Ney's social behavior in Austin was as unorthodox as ever it had been in Hempstead, but in the relatively cosmopolitan capital city her eccentricity won her friends rather than enemies. Short of cash, she impudently wrote to a woman she had never met, Mrs. Sarah Marshall Pease, the widow of a former Texas governor and Austin's reigning social arbiter, asking to borrow a hundred dollars or so. Mrs. Pease received the forwarded letter while away from Austin on vacation and ignored it. When she returned to her family estate, Woodlawn, she learned from her caretaker that Miss Ney had paid a personal visit—that is, the artist had been caught clambering over the fence. "She said she was just looking about," the caretaker reported to

Mrs. Pease, "because she was going to see a lot of the place after you got back."

Whatever umbrage Mrs. Pease might have taken soon melted when Elisabet Ney called again. Charmed by the sculptor's unconventionality, Mrs. Pease extended not only the loan but also an invitation to Miss Ney to spend her weekends at Woodlawn. Miss Ney accepted conditionally. "I must be provided with a hammock to sleep in, and at the table at which I eat no meat must be served. I've been for many years a vegetarian, and now even to sit at a table where human beings are devouring the flesh of dead animals is for me most nauseating." Mrs. Pease eagerly agreed.

Now firmly established in Texas high society and with her artistic fame rapidly spreading throughout America, Elisabet Ney seldom lacked commissions. Her income was not enormous, but it was sufficient to relieve Edmund and herself of their nagging financial worries. Miss Ney could even afford the leisure to model a work for herself alone—a statue of Lady Macbeth, depicted sleepwalking after murdering King Duncan. The sculpture was unquestionably her masterpiece. Miss Ney herself, in her inimitable manner, found the statue so unbearably beautiful that she could not look at it for more than a few minutes a day.

During her golden twilight years, her conduct, far from mellowing, became ever more eccentric—and continued to endear her to rich and famous people. She welcomed to her studio a steady stream of distinguished visitors. Among them were the pianist Paderewski, the dancer Pavlova and singers Enrico Caruso and Ernestine Schumann-Heink. Miss Ney and Madame Schumann-Heink instantly liked each other, and soon after the singer departed, the sculptor wrote to her in a typically pert and familiar manner: "If you appear before your audience tonight wearing a train, I shall come up on the stage and cut it off. I shall have scissors with me. I can't think of a better chance to exemplify my belief in simple natural dress for women. So please wear the longest train you have." The note prompted Madame Schumann-Heink to give her concert in a gown with a hem six inches above the floor.

Miss Ney traveled to Europe in 1895, the first of three return visits. Her reception made it clear she could resume her career in Germany as if she had never left. But she did not want Germany; her home and her

Elisabet Ney, known as "the founder of
art in Texas," finishes a bust of William
Jennings Bryan in her Austin studio in
1900. A statue of Stephen F. Austin,
an early Texas leader, stands behind her.

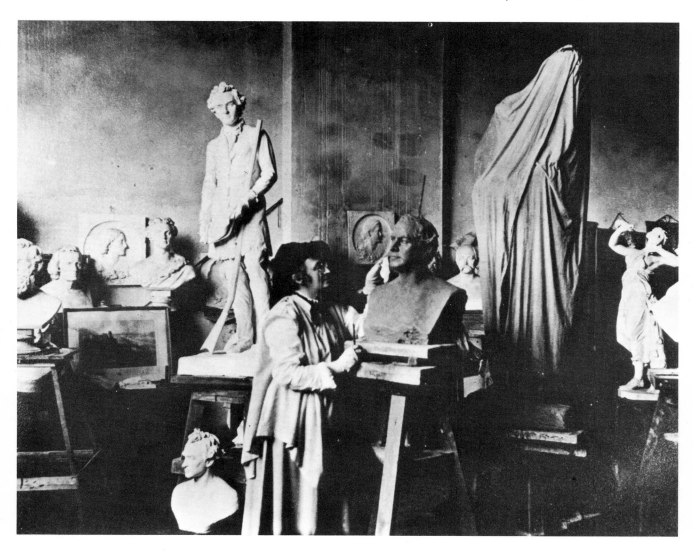

heart by now were in Texas. As her homeward-bound
ship entered the Gulf of Mexico, Miss Ney, sitting in a
steamer chair watching the sunrise, wrote to a friend,
"I'm at this moment experiencing a feeling of expansion
such as I have never known before. Though I am truly
void of what one would call patriotism the appellation
Texas has a charm of a peculiar kind, such as the name
of no other part of the wide earth."

Elisabet Ney died of heart disease in 1907 at 74.
She was buried at Liendo under a live-oak tree that she
and Edmund had planted to shade their last resting
place. He was buried beside her four years later.

Miss Ney's following of Texas admirers paid her
many tributes. They joined together and turned her

studio in Austin into an art museum, a living memorial.

A Texas editor declared, "An account of the present state of art in Texas is chiefly an account of
our great sculptor, Elisabet Ney. It is needless to
ask by what unexpected beneficence of fortune an artist, who was the glory of the most cultured art center of
Europe, was vouchsafed to an obscure young State.
God loves Texas; let that suffice to explain so delightful a miracle."

Elisabet Ney had made another contribution, hardly
less miraculous, just by living her obdurately nonconformist life. She was, as she claimed proudly, a revolu-
tionary, forcing people to accept her on her own terms.
In so doing, she paved the way for kindred spirits.

Sadie Austin stands at ease with her guns on her father's Nebraska ranch, where she worked as a cowgirl. By 1900, when this photograph was taken, many Western women were more at home on the range than in the kitchen.

Dead coyotes lie at the feet of the Wyoming woman who shot them—either to protect her sheep or supplement the family's income. Although fur traders sniffed at the coyote's pelt, counties paid a bounty on the predators.

Lucille Mulhall, a star in her father's Wild West show, ropes four horses and their riders at an Oregon rodeo. With skills developed on her family's Oklahoma ranch, she astonished audiences by competing with men—and winning.

6 | Women with a cause

For many Western women, pioneering did not end with the conquest of a savage land. They had helped tame the frontier; now they were determined to have a hand in shaping its future. Alone and in groups, they became forces for social change—to the frequent bemusement and occasional anger of a male-dominated society.

Sarah Winnemucca, an Indian, passionately denounced the federal Indian Bureau's policies toward her people. Abigail Scott Duniway was a drumbeater for women's suffrage, publishing her own newspaper for the cause, while other women lobbied state legislatures in behalf of the same goal.

But the most visible of the many causes embraced by the new breed of female reformers was surely the temperance movement. Operating under the banner of the Woman's Christian Temperance Union, women launched spirited assaults on saloons, the refuge of much of the male population. And a few—like Carry Nation, who waged a one-woman campaign against Kansas booze parlors—became enduring symbols of female determination. Men angered by attacks on their cherished saloons (*right*) sometimes sloshed their beloved beer onto the sidewalks to prevent bands of women from kneeling in prayer at the entrances.

The temperance goal of national prohibition was not realized until January 16, 1919, but by the end of the century many Western women had won the right to cast a ballot and some were even holding public office.

Damp but undaunted, fervent female temperance boosters continue their siege of a Minnesota saloon in 1878. Minutes earlier the owner's wife had doused them with a pitcher of water from an upper window.

Shaping the future of the West they helped to win

Thomas Dimsdale, the gentleman-editor of the *Montana Post* in the mid-1860s, deferred to no man in his high regard for women. "As sisters, mothers, nurses, friends, sweethearts, and wives," he wrote, "they are the salt of the earth, the sheet anchor of society, and the humanizing and purifying element in humanity. As such they cannot be too much respected, loved and protected."

In any other role, however, they could not be tolerated. So far as Dimsdale was concerned, the salt of the earth belonged in the home: no need for women to step outside to do their purifying. It was deplorable enough for the occasional bold-spirited female to overstep the bounds of convention to indulge her own peculiar whim; it was unthinkable for crusading women to enter public life and actually attempt to change the very way society was run. The mere idea of female reformers was so abhorrent to Dimsdale that he felt driven to plea to the Almighty. "From Blue Stockings, Bloomers, and strong-minded she-males generally," he thundered in the *Post*, "GOOD LORD, DELIVER US."

Dimsdale was not alone in his Victorian attitudes and heartfelt prayers. But a great many other men of the frontier were quite willing to grant a share of public life to the women who had helped them tame the wilderness. Indeed, the single most remarkable phenomenon in the story of Western women is that most of them won the right to vote—a right that had to be accorded them by men—well ahead of their Eastern sisters. Before 1900, four Western states—Wyoming, Colorado, Idaho and Utah—had given the ballot to women.

Moreover, the West chalked up an impressive series of other firsts in recognition of women's abilities beyond the sphere of home. In 1870 Esther Morris of South Pass City, Wyoming Territory, became the nation's first woman justice of the peace. In the same year Wyoming empaneled the first women jurors in the country. In 1887 Susanna Salter of Argonia, Kansas, became the first woman mayor in the United States. The honor of electing the nation's first all-female municipal government—a mayor and five councilwomen—fell to Oskaloosa, Kansas, in 1888. The first woman to achieve statewide elective office was Estelle Reel, who in 1894 became superintendent of public instruction in the new state of Wyoming.

A record such as this argues not only amplitude of vision in the male but also commendable initiative in the female. Unquestionably, the experience of pioneering gave Western women the self-confidence to test themselves. And, though most of the great reform causes they espoused—justice for oppressed minorities, temperance, women's rights and equal suffrage—had originated in the East, the flexibility of Western society permitted them a scope for action denied their Eastern counterparts. Institutions in the young West had not yet hardened into immutability, nor had the individual lost that soul-expanding Western sense of unlimited possibilities. If the covered-wagon mother was often too exhausted or too busy for fresh challenges, her daughters were not. The women of the West gave themselves to their various causes with missionary zeal—winning some, losing some, but on the whole influencing American attitudes and institutions on a wide and permanent scale.

Of all the crusades transported to the frontier lands by women, one in particular struck deep into the very heart of the male domain and so appalled men as to

Saloon-smasher Carry Nation is led away by a town marshal after destroying a tavern in Kansas. Although her violence dismayed less truculent temperance leaders, her tactics caught and held the public eye.

Teetotalers gather in Lawrence, Kansas—on the site of a former beer garden—for a national temperance meeting in September 1878. For more than a week, thousands signed abstinence pledges, heard speeches and called for legislation "to prevent rum suckers from leading youth astray."

make them forever leery of any reform movement promoted by females.

Its primary objective was the saloon—sacrosanct purlieu of the miners, the merchants, the soldiers, the railroaders, the loggers and cowboys, and the rest of the hard-drinking lot that made up the predominantly masculine society of the Old West. Temperance was its name, and it was one of the first causes to enlist the energies of Western women, whose lives were closely and often disastrously affected by the excesses of their men in the use of alcohol.

The torch was carried west by women like Sarah Pellet, who arrived in California from Boston in 1855 with the announced intention of supporting herself by giving temperance lectures. Since she dressed in bloomer costume—a short skirt worn over loose trousers gathered at the ankles, named for feminist Amelia Bloomer, who had made the garb famous—she had little difficulty in attracting gatherings. "No dog fight ever drew together such a crowd," an eyewitness reported of her lecture in the gold-mining town of Weaverville. Sarah proposed a deal to her gaping audience: if they would outlaw liquor, she would return to New England and bring back thousands of young girls to be the wives of temperate Californians. But a drink in hand was more comforting than a bird 3,000 miles away, and no bargain was struck.

Twenty years later a more serious threat arrived, this time a veritable gale blowing out of Ohio, where an antisaloon prayer crusade had sprung up in several towns during the winter of 1873 and spread rapidly as far as the Pacific. In Oregon the atmosphere began stirring in February 1874, and was thoroughly agitated by March. Several Portland ministers conducted antiliquor church meetings, a Women's Temperance Prayer League was formed, and a Great Crusade was launched against the evils of alcohol.

Since Portland was blessed with a staggering density of licensed liquor outlets—one for every 40 citizens, counting women and children—the reformers' first move was a public appeal to the owners to close their doors. Simultaneously the crusaders began circulating an abstinence pledge and quickly racked up more than 1,100 names. "The women seem everywhere to be lifted up out of themselves," wrote one lady to a friend, "and to be moved with a very powerful influence."

So uplifted were the women that they decided upon stronger measures: crusaders must advance to the enemy lines, and pray and sing their hymns inside the saloons themselves. An exciting, troubling time followed in Portland. Ladies were arrested for disturbing the peace, then freed on grounds that they were exercising freedom of worship. Brave outriders encountered humiliating insult, like the two women who stepped into the Webfoot Saloon one day—only intending, as it happened, to collect abstinence signatures—and were met head on by a man with fire in his eye, saloon owner Walter Moffett.

"Without giving them time to announce their errand," wrote crusade chronicler Frances Fuller Victor, describing the events of that stirring spring in a little book entitled *The Women's War on Whisky*, "he seized each rudely by an arm, and thrust them into the street, exclaiming, 'Get out of this! I keep a respectable house and don't want any d----d wh---s here.' "

After this shocking encounter, the Webfoot Saloon became one of the hottest targets for the temperance warriors. Groups of indignant ladies called upon Moffett almost daily and demanded entrance to his place. When, as expected, the saloonkeeper kept turning them away, the crusaders launched into lively sessions of saying prayers and singing hymns outside the Webfoot, effectively putting a damper on the spirits of the customers within and driving the proprietor into a frenzy. Eventually a harassed and worn-out Moffett closed up his establishment. But victory over an occasional saloonkeeper was not much comfort when a slate of temperance candidates was soundly defeated in Portland's 1874 election.

The movement was not dead, however. In that same year the Woman's Christian Temperance Union was founded, again in rumbustious Ohio. Soon afterward the WCTU acquired a brilliant leader: Frances Willard, a daughter of the middle frontier whose family had traveled to the West by covered wagon to pioneer in Wisconsin Territory in 1846. Under the guidance of Frances Willard the WCTU became, in the West as in the East, a vehicle that drew many basically conservative women out of the home and organized them into an effective social force.

One WCTU member, Carry Nation, was a redoubtable force in herself. Born in 1846 and brought up in Kentucky, Texas and Missouri by a half-mad mother and a strongly religious father, Carry Nation was the very epitome of the type of woman from whom the Thomas Dimsdales of the West called upon the Good Lord for deliverance.

According to Carry's own account of her crusade, *The Use and Need of the Life of Carry A. Nation*, her loathing of strong drink was born when she realized shortly after her first wedding that her husband was a hopeless drunkard. Six months after she left him and returned to her parents' home to bear his child, he died of the effects of alcoholism. Her second marriage, to a lawyer and minister much older than she, was also a joyless union, for David Nation abstained as much from love as from liquor. Later Carry would claim that the Almighty had denied her domestic happiness because He had a higher mission for her: to take the field defending the homes of others. But her crusade was no mere idiosyncrasy; it came at a time when alcoholism was a severe and widespread social problem that was a deep concern not only to women but also to a great number of men.

Carry's call to direct action against liquor came first in Medicine Lodge, Kansas, where the Nations settled in 1889. Kansas had been legally dry since 1880, but drinkers hoodwinked the law by swilling whiskey "for medicinal purposes" in the back rooms of drugstores or hanging out in clubs where tippling was an open secret. Carry helped organize a local group of WCTU crusaders and tried to rouse public opinion through denunciations delivered by David Nation from his pulpit— Carry having told him what to preach. She herself rose in church and named the miscreants who were selling and drinking liquor, and then she rebuked them to their faces in the streets.

Finally, in 1899, when she was in her fifties, she resorted to the tactics used years earlier by the crusaders in Portland: with a women supporter she marched to the Medicine Lodge liquor joint of one Mart Strong and, as her companion played the hand organ, she sallied into the bar singing a temperance song. A festive crowd gathered outside to watch the fun. When the proprietor ordered Carry to leave, she refused to budge. "I continued to sing," she recollected, "with tears running down my face." Strong finally took firm hold of the resisting Carry and maneuvered her out onto the

sidewalk—none too daintily perhaps, for she was a sturdily built woman nearly six feet tall—where the enthralled onlookers responded with yells of support for the abused Mrs. Nation.

Stung into action by the commotion, the city officials decided to close Mart Strong's illegal establishment; and the defeated saloonkeeper left town. Carry and her associates, using similar procedures, went on to close down the remaining bars. By March 1900, Medicine Lodge became as dry in fact as in theory, and Carry was a local legend.

Under divine guidance, as she thought, Carry selected her next target: Kiowa, a town 20 miles away on the Oklahoma border to which the frustrated drinkers of Medicine Lodge has resorted to buy booze from bootleggers. One day, she armed herself secretly with brickbats and rocks, drove her buggy to Kiowa, stayed overnight with a friend and next day strode to Dobson's Saloon. "I am going to break up this den of vice," she announced to Dobson, and heaved her missiles at bottles, mirrors and glassware with fine effect. Gusting

out of Dobson's she went briskly to work on several other saloons; and before the dumbfounded Kiowans could decide what to do with her, she was back in her buggy headed toward Medicine Lodge.

All this was mere prelude to her historic assault on the Hotel Carey barroom in Wichita. The Carey's illicit drinking establishment prided itself on its luxurious appointments: a curving bar of fine cherry-wood, a huge expanse of mirror and an enormous oil painting depicting *Cleopatra at the Bath*. Two days after Christmas 1900, Carry sailed into the bar. "Glory to God! Peace on earth, good will to men," she exclaimed, heaving stones at the shamelessly naked Cleopatra and the expensive mirror, which cost $1,500. As the astonished bartender and early-morning drinkers recoiled in dismay, she whipped an iron rod and a cane from her skirts and vigorously tore into everything within reach until the police arrived. "You put me in here a cub," shouted Carry from her jail cell, after being charged with malicious destruction of property, "but I will go out a roaring lion and make all hell howl."

Two weeks later—the charge against her having been dropped by the prosecution—she was out and in full roar. By now, newspapers had made her famous coast to coast. That very month, a state temperance convention meeting in Topeka invited her to make an address and awarded her a gold medal inscribed "To the Bravest Woman in Kansas." Next, with David Nation in tow, Carry called on the governor and lectured him for not enforcing the prohibition law. But the elderly Mr. Nation's enthusiasm was lagging, and soon he told Carry it was time to stop all this and come back to Medicine Lodge. When she declined, he went home alone and later that year successfully sued for divorce on grounds of desertion. Carry relieved her feelings by leading a smashers' brigade against Topeka's famous Senate Bar, a favorite rendezvous of legislators, where her hatchet—which she had recently discovered to be an incomparably effective bar-wrecking tool—sent shards and splinters flying in all directions.

Hard pressed for funds after emerging from another brief sojourn in jail, Carry took to the lecture trail. From this point on, she spent more time declaiming

ally smashed up the stage-set saloon, many turned away from her in disapproval. The national WCTU, after much soul-searching, declined to endorse her. Nevertheless, a great many persons the country over felt she was doing noble, desperately needed work and faithfully sent her their nickels and dimes to continue her crusade. Carry, sincerely committed to her cause, never spent the money on anything else.

Carry's last hatchetation was in Butte, Montana, where in January 1910 she entered the Windsor dance hall and advanced menacingly toward one of the nude paintings. Before she could strike a blow, the proprietor, May Maloy, intercepted her and unceremoniously gave Carry the heave-ho. Perhaps what utterly deflated the vanquished Carry was to be manhandled by a woman. Aging, tiring, she hung up her hatchet, and 18 months later she was dead at 64. The inscription on her tombstone read: "She hath done what she could." Eight years after her death the Eighteenth Amendment brought nationwide prohibition.

Sharing Carry Nation's conviction that new laws could solve old problems were women with a very different cause—crusaders on behalf of a people deprived of human rights. Some remarkable Western women, including two Indians, played crucial roles in stirring the nation's conscience to a more humanitarian concern for the Indian, which they hoped ultimately would be expressed in law.

Years of pitched battles fought in the West between white men and Indians, climaxed by the Battle of the Little Bighorn in 1876, clearly evidenced the utter bankruptcy of federal Indian policy. Yet not until attention was focused on one isolated act of folly and injustice by the government was public indignation aroused and long overdue reforms undertaken.

The episode involved the Ponca Indians, a small Plains tribe that two decades earlier had agreed to stay on the path of peace in exchange for a treaty guaranteeing them—"during good behavior"—possession of the lands they inhabited along the Nebraska-Dakota border. Subsequently, Washington officialdom decided it had made a mistake, for certain of those lands turned out to be claimed by the Sioux, a big, belligerent tribe in need of some placating. The government chose expedience. In 1877 the order went out to move the Poncas

from public platforms and stages than on actual "hatchetations," as she called the smashing forays with her favorite weapon. Grandmotherly Carry in her long, black alpaca dress and bonnet, with a raised hatchet in one hand and an open Bible in the other, became as familiar a personage to Americans as suffragette Susan B. Anthony or singer Lillian Russell.

But when Carry Nation took to selling souvenir hatchets at prices ranging from 25 cents to 50 cents, and even appeared in vaudeville stunts such as a version of *Ten Nights in a Barroom* in which she person-

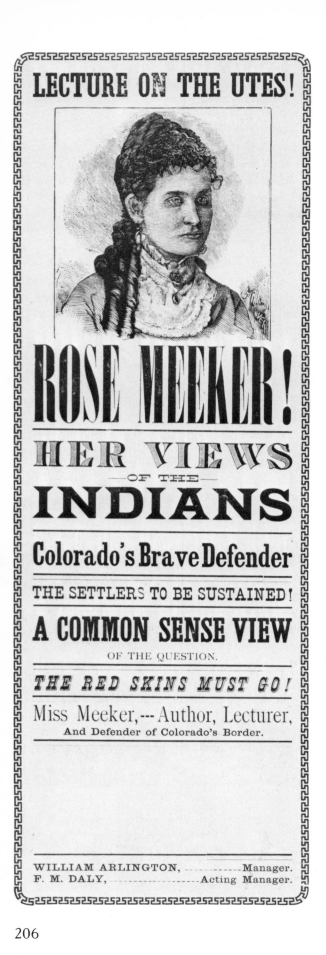

A Denver poster announces a lecture by Rose Meeker, whose father was killed and mother and sister kidnapped by Utes in 1879. Her speeches countered growing liberal sympathy for the Indians' plight.

to Indian Territory (present-day eastern Oklahoma). Bitter but peaceable, the Poncas allowed themselves to be herded south on a debilitating 500-mile march by units of the United States Army.

In their new location, the uprooted and disheartened tribe fell victim to malaria, which killed off more than one third of the 700 people who had made the trek south. Among those who died was the 16-year-old son of Standing Bear, the Ponca chief. The youth's dying request to his father was to be buried at home. And so, with some 30 followers and the body of his son, Standing Bear headed back north in 1879.

After an arduous 10-week journey the little band, weary, ailing and half starved, reached the eastern Nebraska reservation of the friendly Omahas, who were closely related to the Poncas by intermarriage. Omaha Chief Joseph La Flesche—son of a French fur trader and an Indian woman of Ponca-Omaha blood—persuaded the Poncas to remain with him on the Omaha reservation for the time needed to recover enough strength to travel.

But the Poncas had barely arrived when an Army unit, on orders from Washington, came to take the runaways to the fort at Omaha, preliminary to shunting them back to Indian Territory. Taking with him the box containing the bones of his son, Standing Bear trudged with his band to Omaha—where all were placed under arrest for leaving Indian Territory.

The Poncas' plight did not go unnoticed. An Omaha newspaperman named Thomas Tibbles learned of the Indians' troubles through a sympathetic Army general. After visiting Standing Bear in confinement and coming away appalled by the bureaucratic crassness that had placed him there, Tibbles wrote a series of articles in the *Omaha Herald* urging freedom for the prisoners. No one read his stories with more interest than Susette La Flesche, daughter of the Omaha chief.

Susette, born in 1854, had been educated at a Presbyterian girls' seminary in New Jersey and was now teaching at a school run by the government on the Omaha reservation. She was articulate, literate, as fluent in English as in her tribal language, well versed in the saga of the Poncas and deeply concerned with their misfortunes.

Susette wrote a lengthy letter to Tibbles, chronicling the Ponca story as she knew it. Using this addi-

Sarah Winnemucca appears in the Great Plains Indian garb she wore while pleading her cause—the granting of land to the Paiutes—during the 1880s. Although the press made her famous, she was unable to get the federal government to act. Disillusioned, she spent her last years teaching.

Photographed in Boston, a city much moved by her 1879 crusade, Omaha Indian Susette La Flesche's demureness belies her zeal for exposing injustice to Indians. She lectured as far away as England.

Helen Clarke meets Indians arriving at the Ponca reservation in Oklahoma to receive land allotments in the 1890s. The daughter of a white trader and a Blackfoot mother, Miss Clarke was one of the few women who helped manage the federal Indian program. Some Indians complained that the "Great Father" sent a woman to do a man's work.

211

overpowered. One of the captives was her father. Encountering a patrol of soldiers, Sarah immediately volunteered her services to the Army. Its most urgent need, she learned, was for scouts to find the Bannock war party and spy out its strength. She volunteered; two Paiutes joined her.

After a day and a half of tracking, Sarah and her companions located their quarry some 100 miles away in eastern Oregon. Disguising herself in a blanket and war paint, the Paiute woman slipped into the bustling Bannock camp unnoticed. She reached her father's lodge and outlined a plan of escape. That evening the captive Paiute women managed to escape from the camp, pretending they were going to gather wood for the night. While the Bannocks relaxed over a meal, Sarah, her father and several hundred Paiute braves filtered out of the camp in small groups. They joined their women, mounted horses that had been stealthily cut from the grazing Bannock herd and rode for their lives. Approximately half were recaptured by pursuing Bannocks, but the others reached the safety of an Army encampment a day and a half away.

Sarah's daring feat, and the useful information it produced, so impressed General Oliver O. Howard that he recommended her for a $500 reward and persuaded her to be his personal interpreter and guide for the duration of the Bannock war. Sarah's brave conduct throughout the arduous six-week campaign made her the darling of newspaper reporters; and when the war ended, she was famous.

But for the Paiutes in general, the Bannock war turned out to be disastrous. Promised return to the Malheur Reservation, they were marched instead to a prisoner-of-war camp at Yakima in Washington Territory. The duped tribe blamed Sarah. As a war heroine she might have escaped their fate; instead she chose to accompany them to Yakima and fight for tolerable living conditions. When some money owed her by the military arrived, she used it to travel to San Francisco and make an appeal to the public on behalf of her people.

In San Francisco her lectures attracted large audiences curious to see the spirited Indian woman who had been an Army scout. They found themselves captivated by her impassioned protests against the Paiutes' mistreatment. A physician who attended one of Sarah's lectures described her with nice precision as "nearly beautiful," and he was impressed to find her "expressing herself perfectly in good English, able to translate quite naturally the most intimate feelings of her soul. She did it with such passion and conviction, she had such pathetic emotions, that many people were moved to tears."

Sarah's outspoken criticism of the Indian bureau and its agents got full play in the San Francisco press. One result was an invitation to Washington, at bureau expense, to discuss tribal conditions in person. Sarah, her father, a brother and a cousin made the trip in January 1880. Somewhat to her surprise, Interior Secretary Carl Schurz—who was regarded by reformers as conservative to the point of indifference in his approach to Indian affairs—readily gave them a signed executive order authorizing the Paiutes' release from Yakima plus a grant to each adult male of 160 acres of land at Malheur. The Winnemuccas were even allowed a quick meeting with President Rutherford B. Hayes, who expressed his gratification that they had received what they had come for.

But at Yakima the presiding Indian agent refused to recognize the government order; it was not, he said, personally addressed to him and, besides, the release of the Paiutes would incite white settlers and cause blood to spill. Sarah quickly wrote to the Secretary of the Interior and telegraphed the President, but she never received replies. Humiliated and disgusted, she withdrew from public life.

By 1883 she was back in the campaign, having been invited East by the reformers in Boston to present her people's case. Clad in deerskin richly fringed with shell beads, red leather leggings and a crown of red leather trimmed with stars, Sarah presented as appealing a figure as had Susette La Flesche when visiting Boston a few years before.

Sarah's lectures were received with such interest that she was persuaded to write a book, which was published later in the year as *Life Among the Paiutes*. On the tide of a swelling current of interest in her cause, Sarah and her Boston sponsors circulated a petition demanding that the government grant the Paiutes land. Massachusetts' Senator Dawes was the sponsoring legislator, and in 1884 the bill passed Congress. Sarah, now about 40 years old, returned to her people,

Biddy Mason: from slave to benefactress

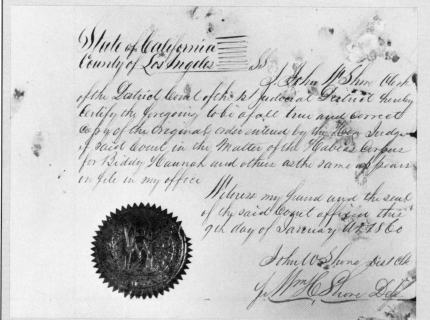

In 1860 Biddy Mason obtained a certified copy of the order that had set her free.

Few Western women had more reason to value hard-won freedom than Biddy Mason did. Born a slave in 1818, she was taken to California in 1851. California was a free state, but she was held in servitude until 1856, when a judge heard of her case and ordered her release.

Free at last, Biddy vowed to be an inspiration and help to her people. With money earned working as a nurse, she bought a house. More acquisitions followed, and Biddy used her funds to assist the needy. She aided hard-pressed black churches, and in the 1880s she paid grocery bills for families left homeless by a flood. Years after her death in 1891, a book of black history hailed Biddy Mason as "the most remarkable pioneer of color coming to California."

Biddy Mason (*in doorway, left*), affectionately known as "Grandma Mason," visits with her friends and family in Los Angeles.

A SUFFRAGE AWAKENING IN ART

Awash with its creator's belief in spiritualism, an allegorical painting called *The Sleeping Giantess (above)* was one Western woman's contribution to the equal suffrage movement. The artist, Lavinia Gertrude Waterhouse, hoped the picture would instruct viewers about the votes-for-women cause. Using Yosemite Valley as a metaphor for the United States, she peopled the painting with a wide cast of characters, real and symbolic. The specter of Abraham Lincoln looks on benignly, and the Goddess of Liberty stands in the sleep-strewn hair of the dozing giantess, who represents politically unconcerned women, while suffragettes climb the mountain to awaken her.

a heroine again, addressed by the Paiutes as "Mother."

But then came a crushing setback. Interior Secretary Schurz neglected to implement the legislation, and the new Congress elected soon afterward was too absorbed with other concerns to press the matter. Nor did Sarah Winnemucca's Paiutes benefit from Senator Dawes's general Indian reform legislation, passed three years later, in 1887. Nothing whatever, in spite of Sarah's efforts, was done to right the injustices committed against the Paiutes.

Sarah's disillusionment, after repeated betrayals, was complete; and this time her retirement from public life was permanent. After several years of ill-health she died in 1891, not yet 50, thinking herself—as her people thought her—a failure. Yet, in the long run, she was not a failure. Inspired by her monumental efforts, later generations of Paiutes battled victoriously before courts and government agencies to protect and increase their holdings of land—at a time when other Indian tribes were dispersing. In their hard-won success, Sarah Winnemucca's tribesmen could at last appreciate the magnitude of what she had tried to do.

Politically, American women themselves were something of an oppressed group in the 19th Century: they were voteless—except in those areas where men and women had worked together to achieve women's suffrage. Fittingly, it was on the frontier that women first captured the right to vote. Indeed, Wyoming Territory was the first government in the world to grant women political equality, in 1869.

It was men, of course, who gave the women of Wyoming the vote, but much of the credit for their decision can be attributed to a forceful woman named Esther Hobart McQuigg Morris, known in Wyoming as "the Mother of Woman Suffrage."

Esther Morris in 1869 was a 55-year-old woman who early that year had traveled to Wyoming from Illinois to join her husband and two grown sons in the booming gold camp of South Pass City. Nearly six feet tall and weighing 180 pounds, with a countenance aptly described as craggy, Mrs. Morris was as strong-minded as she looked—and her mind was firmly set on equal rights for women.

The women of the East had given her precedent and inspiration enough for her cause: as early as 1848, Eastern feminists had convened at Seneca Falls, New York, and delivered a general declaration of women's rights—including the right to vote. They were only too well aware, however, that their rights were circumscribed by entrenched traditions, whereas the West represented a clean slate upon which the progressive idea of sexual equality could be inscribed and incorporated into territorial and state constitutions yet unwritten. To Mrs. Morris the outlook for women's suffrage seemed promising in the wide-open political climate of Wyoming; and as the time approached for the newly opened territory to form a government, she went into action for her cause.

Accounts of her tactics vary, but one version has it that Mrs. Morris invited opposing candidates from her district to a tea party immediately before the fall election and, by playing off one politician against the other, extracted promises from both to support women's suffrage in the new legislature. Another account claims

that William H. Bright, who was to be the successful candidate, listened sympathetically to Mrs. Morris because she had assisted his wife through a difficult childbirth and probably saved her life. Still another story says that Mrs. Bright, too, was a suffragette and that her indulgent husband, a transplanted Virginian, was particularly receptive to the joint urgings of the two women because he saw no reason why his wife should be denied the ballot if exslaves could vote.

In any case, when the legislature convened, Bright introduced the enfranchising bill, and in spite of some dissenting voices, it was passed—supposedly, according to political hindsight, because the founding fathers of scantily populated Wyoming believed its passage would publicize the new territory and encourage women to settle there. Antisuffrage forces tried to pressure the territorial governor into vetoing the bill. But the governor signed the measure into law. Legend has it that, on that history-making occasion, the men of Wyoming proposed a toast: "Lovely ladies, once our superiors, now our equals." Because women were now on the voters' rolls they would also serve on juries for the first time. The same legislature also passed laws ensuring personal property rights for wives and parity of pay for male and female teachers.

Men in other parts of the country viewed the developments in Wyoming with interest—and some amusement. The appointment of Esther Morris as justice of the peace in boisterous South Pass City, early in 1870, brought on a blizzard of derisive comments and cartoons in the Eastern press. Mrs. Morris herself saw no humor in the situation and discharged her duties with such aplomb and skill that not one of her more than 40 decisions was reversed on appeal. Later in the year, when the first jury in the world to include women convened in Laramie, a contingent of the Eastern press arrived to caricature the proceedings. The people of Wyoming stood firm. "You shall not be driven by the sneers, jeers and insults of a laughing crowd from the temple of justice," said the presiding judge to his female jurors. He meant it; and they were not.

In 1890 when Wyoming was seeking admission to the Union, the women's suffrage clause in its proposed state constitution met considerable opposition in the U.S. Congress, for no state had yet given full women's suffrage. When matters seemed at an impasse, some

Ann Eliza Webb Young was the first Mormon wife to openly denounce polygamy. Her divorce from Brigham Young and her book, *Wife No. 19,* roused public enmity toward Mormon marital practices.

Wyoming women wired the territory's representative in Washington, giving him permission to withdraw the clause if necessary. They said they were confident that once Wyoming was a state, the men of Wyoming would give them back their vote. With equal gallantry, the men refused their offer. "We will remain out of the Union a hundred years," the Wyoming legislature declared, "rather than come in without the women."

On March 26, 1890, the bill to admit Wyoming squeaked through the House. Three months later the Senate also approved, and in July the President affixed his signature. When Wyoming celebrated its statehood on July 23, 1890, Esther Morris was among the honored pioneers who took part in the ceremonies: she had been chosen to present to the governor of the 44th state a 44-star flag made by the women of Wyoming.

To the astonishment of a nation that imagined Mormon wives to be no more than harem slaves, the women of Utah Territory were given the vote only months after it was granted to the self-reliant females of Wyoming. Oddly enough, it was the issue of polygamy that precipitated the granting of female suffrage in Utah—and the same issue later caused it to be revoked.

The concept of plural marriage was so detestable to non-Mormons that, as early as the 1860s, political action had begun in Congress to stamp it out. The stratagem of Indiana Congressman George Washington Julian was particularly ingenious—or so he no doubt believed. Julian, in 1869, introduced a bill to Congress that would give the women of Utah the right to vote, reasoning that Mormon women, who outnumbered their men by a ratio of 3 to 2, would take advantage of their ballots to rise up en masse and outlaw polygamy at the polls.

Brigham Young and the other Mormon leaders knew better. They were convinced that even if Mormon women were to be enfranchised, the vast majority of them would remain loyal to their church, which preached plural marriage as essential to eternal happiness. And so, in 1870, before Congress could act, the Utah territorial legislature stole a march on Washington and itself granted the vote to women. Not only did this clever move refute the accusation that Mormon women were voiceless chattels but it also gave the church more ballots with which to maintain control of Utah, where a growing number of non-Mormons had begun to settle.

The Mormon women duly went to the polls and, as Brigham Young had predicted, faithfully supported their men. Enemies of the Mormon Church, far from being reassured that Mormon women were happy with their lot, claimed that plural wives kowtowed to their husbands and meekly cast their ballots as church elders dictated. "When Mormon women vote it is simply duplicating the male vote over and over again," a hostile writer alleged. "They all vote the same ticket—the one given them."

Adding her voice to the rising tide of antipathy toward Mormon marriage practices was Ann Eliza Webb Young, a rebellious wife of the prophet Brigham Young himself. Her personal crusade against polygamy was curiously intertwined with the cause of women's suffrage in Utah.

Ann Eliza Webb had grown up in Mormonism and in polygamy, her father having taken a second wife

216

Utah's industrious silk makers, toiling for the church

In his sometimes utopian efforts to build a self-sustaining community on the plains of Utah, Mormon leader Brigham Young called upon the faith's women to raise silkworms and weave the silk into fabric for their own dresses. The money the women might otherwise spend for fashionable silk garments from outsiders, Young reasoned, would thus stay in the Mormon community.

Silk production in Utah began in earnest in 1877, when the Mormon Female Relief Society organized local silk associations for disseminating silkworm eggs and information on what to do with them. Within a year, Mormon women were tending five million silkworms in trays stacked from floor to ceiling against the walls of their parlors and bedrooms. Even children took part, gathering mulberry leaves from the hundreds of trees planted to supply food for the worms.

Enthusiasm for the project yielded some astonishing results: Sister Christine Forsgren of Brigham City produced 130 yards of silk in her home in the early 1880s; another ambitious woman started her silkworks with three ounces rather than the customary one ounce of silkworm eggs, and a few months later she had to evacuate her house to accommodate the 160,000 growing worms.

Most of the Mormon women's silk operations, however, were contained in one or two rooms. They produced handkerchiefs, stockings, thread and lace goods. One of Brigham Young's wives and a daughter "each wore a beautiful dress made from local silk" at the 1893 Chicago World's Columbian exposition, reported the Utah Silk Association.

Although in the long run the silk produced at home proved unable to compete in price with the imported product, the Mormon women kept the industry alive for 28 years as a duty to their church. Most shared the belief of Sister Eyring of the St. George Relief Society that "we will get our reward, whether we make much or little." In 1906 the church decided the effort was futile and the local silk associations were dissolved.

Mormons in Springfield, Utah, collect silkworm cocoons from tree branches and discard the worms into a tray on the ground.

before she was two years old. When he married three more wives, Ann Eliza was 12, old enough to notice her mother's resentment of a system that she accepted only from a sense of religious duty. "They did not like a polygamous life," said Ann Eliza of her father's wives, "and only endured it because they thought they must."

As Ann Eliza developed into a beautiful young woman, her charms captured the attention of Brigham Young, long a particular friend of her family. Aware of his close scrutiny, she let it be known—in a general way—that she had no intention of becoming a plural wife to any man.

At 18 she impulsively married a sometime actor named James Dee and quickly bore him two sons. In less than three years the marriage foundered. It was Brigham Young who stepped in to expedite a civil divorce. He then set about romancing the reluctant Ann Eliza with every resource at his disposal—including, she later claimed, a threat to bankrupt her brother if she did not capitulate. The prophet was 67 and Ann Eliza was 24 when, in 1869, she finally gave in and became his 19th and last wife. Other reckonings count her as his 27th wife, but whatever the number, she was one wife too many.

She refused to live in the Lion House—which took its name from one of Brigham Young's titles, "the Lion of the Lord"—where many of Young's wives and children resided, and at length the prophet provided her with a dwelling of her own. But even this mark of distinction did not compensate her for what she began to feel was neglect: "He called to see me at my new residence when he could find opportunity, which was not very often." Her dishes, she complained, were old bits of crockery left over from a defunct bakery and the carpet a hand-me-down from the Lion House. To earn some money, she began taking in boarders. The last straw was Young's refusal, one day in 1873, to replace the ailing cookstove on which the boarders' meals were prepared. Ann Eliza took a breathtakingly bold step: she moved out of her house and into a non-Mormon hotel. Within a week she filed suit for divorce, demanding a settlement of $200,000 and legal expenses of $20,000.

Her decampment made stunning news. Instantly she was a national celebrity, overwhelmed by reporters and lecture-booking agents. When she felt brave enough for a public interview in her hotel lobby, she was outspoken in her denunciations of polygamy and of Young. He in turn called her an adulteress and offered a settlement of $15,000, which she refused. In the autumn of 1873 Ann Eliza fled Utah—under dark of night, as if in fear of her life—and traveled secretly to Denver to begin the first of many lecture tours.

All over the country she drew attentive audiences, comporting herself with ladylike circumspection but effectively adding fuel to the fire of antipolygamy sentiment. In the nation's capital, Congress recessed to listen to her, and President and Mrs. Ulysses S. Grant put in an appearance to show interest in her cause. Interested people who could not see Ann Eliza in person read her book, *Wife No. 19, or The Story of a Life in Bondage,* and they gobbled up newspaper accounts of her legal battle to obtain alimony from the prophet. Her efforts to achieve a satisfactory settlement failed; but if it was any consolation to her, Ann Eliza's public outcries against plural marriage helped to stimulate the passage of a federal bill, in 1882, banning polygamy in the territories.

Thereafter, her lecture topic obsolete, Ann Eliza's life story trailed off into obscurity. The Mormons, however, continued to practice plural marriage covertly, and in 1887 Congress, blaming compliant wives, responded by enacting a law that specifically repealed the right of women in Utah Territory to vote.

A drive to regain the ballot soon began; in its forefront was a woman who, unlike Ann Eliza Young, was committed to polygamy but was as firmly committed to the cause of female suffrage. Emmeline Wells of Salt Lake City, a plural wife and the mother of six children, energetically immersed herself in community affairs and held the editorship of the hard-hitting *Woman's Exponent* for nearly 40 years. Through editorials and articles, public appearances before national feminist conventions and vigorous lobbying in Washington, she campaigned in forthright style for the return of the lost franchise, and she went a long way toward dispelling the suspicion of Mormonism and polygamy that Brigham Young's rebellious wife had helped to foster.

Yet she won only half her cause. In 1890 Utah, looking toward statehood, bowed to the inevitable and abolished the doctrine of plural marriage. Statehood was granted in 1896 and, when it came, it included the

A proud editor, Abigail Scott Duniway holds the first run of *The New Northwest* in 1871. Mrs. Duniway often used crime and scandal articles to entice readers into accepting her equal rights point of view.

restoration of women's suffrage—earning for Utah the honor of being among the first four states in the Union to give women the right to vote.

Oregon, by contrast, was admitted to statehood in 1859 but did not extend the right to vote to women for many decades thereafter. That it eventually did so in 1912, eight years before the adoption of the Nineteenth Amendment granted nationwide suffrage to women, was due in large measure to the efforts of Abigail Scott Duniway, one of the first and bravest feminists in the lists.

Abigail Scott was born on her parents' farm in central Illinois in 1834, the second daughter in a family of 12 children. The first baby, a boy, was lost. Abigail was 10 when she learned how disappointed her parents had been when their second child was a girl and how, when she herself came along 17 months later, her

mother's sorrow over the infant's sex was "almost too grievous to be borne." A man on the frontier wanted sons to help him with the heavy farm work, though there was wearying toil enough for daughters if he had them—and little but more of the same for them to look forward to as they grew up. Abigail never forgot the numbing shock of hearing her mother groan at the birth of another little sister, "Poor baby! She'll be a woman some day. A woman's lot is so hard!"

In 1852 Scott sold the Illinois farm over his wife's protests and set out for Oregon with his family and a small party of emigrants in a five-wagon train. Their 2,400-mile trek, which took nearly six months, was marred by tragedy. Abigail's mother—"our gentle, faithful, self-sacrificing mother"—exhausted by 22 years of drudgery and childbearing, fell easy prey to cholera and soon died. Several weeks later the family lost its youngest member, three-year-old Willie, to dysentery. The remaining Scotts, saddened by their losses, arrived in Oregon that fall.

The following spring, 18-year-old Abigail went to work as a schoolteacher in the hamlet of Eola. Her credentials were extremely modest—less than a sixth-grade education in the local log school back in Illinois and a copy of Webster's *Elementary Speller*—but that did not inhibit her.

The young schoolmistress enjoyed her independence, but not so much that she spurned the agreeable masculine attentions coming her way. Females were a rarity in Oregon, and as precious to men as gold dust because of Oregon's Land Donation Act of 1850, which gave each new settler 640 acres if married but only half that if single. Abigail herself had every intention of getting married and raising a family. Before many months passed, "I met my fate," she wrote, "in the person of Mr. Ben C. Duniway." They were married in August 1853, and they settled on Ben's donation claim in Clackamas County.

Young Mrs. Duniway assumed the unending round of toil that was the lot of every pioneer wife and mother, becoming, as she put it, "a general pioneer drudge." She bore two babies within two and a half years of her marriage day, served as cook and laundress to her husband's hired men, played hostess to every hungry, lonely bachelor in the neighborhood who felt like dropping by at mealtime, and made thousands of pounds of but-

Enrolling the press for women's equality

Among the women who founded newspapers to push their political ideals, few approached the enterprise with the temerity of Caroline Churchill. Without funds but never to be outdone, as she said, "in plucky effort," the exteacher got out the first edition of *The Colorado Antelope* in 1879 on credit. By 1882 the feisty Denver monthly had gone weekly and had been renamed *Queen Bee.*

Espousing her own brand of blunderbuss feminism, the crotchety Mrs. Churchill used her paper to rail against men ("the arch enemy of the race"), to push vocational education for girls and to advocate pensions for mothers with dependent children.

Women gained political equality in Colorado in 1893. While it is difficult to measure how big a part the *Queen Bee* actually played in this victory, modesty never stopped the publisher from saluting herself. In her autobiography she stated, "It is not at all likely that another woman on the continent could under the same conditions accomplish as much."

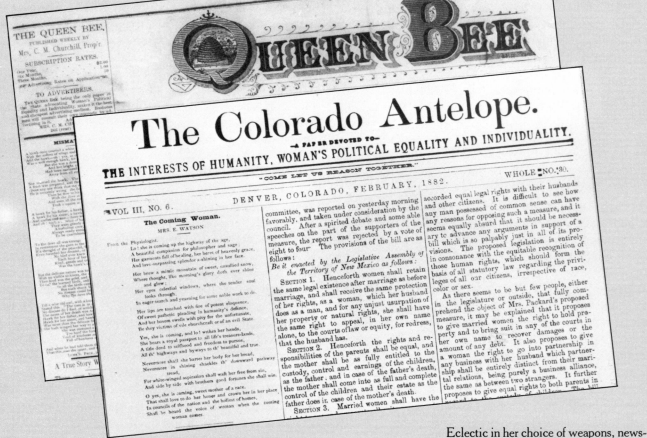

Eclectic in her choice of weapons, newspaper publisher Caroline Churchill used everything from mawkish poetry to serious political reporting in an effort to rally Colorado women behind equal rights.

ter every year, which with her chickens and eggs, she took to the market and exchanged for groceries or sold to cover farm expenses. It was not at all her idea of a permanent career for an independent-minded woman who had earned her own salary before marriage.

But the young Duniways had a goal, and they achieved it: when Ben's four years of probation on his claim ended, he was free to sell it and buy something more to their liking. They moved to a beautifully located farm in Yamhill County that became, Abigail said, "my good husband's pride." Here she bore two more sons and worked, if anything, harder than ever.

Ben, too, toiled to make a success of the farm, but good nature and bad luck were his undoing. One day Abigail listened and watched helplessly—"being a nonentity in law"—while her husband obligingly co-signed three interest-bearing notes for a friend. Months later after crop failures and a Yamhill River flood had brought hard times to the county, the sheriff appeared at the Duniways' door in Ben's absence and served Abigail with a summons for the unpaid notes.

Abigail raged inwardly at the injustice of it all but could only pack up in silence while Ben sold the farm to pay off the notes and interest. The Duniways moved to a little property they owned in the town of Lafayette. They were scarcely settled when Ben had an accident with a runaway team of horses that left him a semi-invalid for the rest of his life. Suddenly it was up to Abigail to support Ben and the children, a challenge she accepted with gusto.

She opened a school in their house and with the money she made, the Duniways were able to move to the larger town of Albany. There Abigail resumed teaching until she could save and borrow enough to finance her next enterprise: a millinery and notions store. The shop was a success. Within three weeks she was able to pay back the money she had borrowed to start it. The Duniways' scramble for financial security was over, and a new phase of Abigail's life had begun.

At her millinery counter, Abigail got some eye-opening glimpses of her customers' predicaments. One weeping woman begged for piecework sewing: she had promised her daughters raincoats if they worked hard making butter, only to see the cash appropriated by her husband to buy a blooded racehorse. A mother of five, left destitute when her husband sold all the family furniture and disappeared, appealed for help to Abigail, through whose good offices a neighboring businessman loaned the woman money to replace her furniture and open a boardinghouse. Just as she was on her feet again, the errant husband reappeared and took legal possession of everything; the wife, of course, lacked any recourse in law to stop him.

"There was nothing left for her but the divorce courts," wrote Abigail. "The family was scattered, my philanthropic neighbor lost his money, and the little religious world of Albany went on sighing over the degeneracy of the times that was making divorces easy. In looking backward, it seems strange to me now that I didn't sooner see the need of votes for women."

She credited her enlightenment to Ben. One evening she was describing a visit she had made to the courthouse that day. Reluctantly (for the courthouse was an all-male preserve, where women drew curious stares), she had accompanied a widow involved in estate matters, who needed a witness to testify to her sound financial character. Abigail's close-up look at the law's inequities had so outraged her that, when she finished telling Ben the story, she burst out: "One-half of the women are dolls, the rest of them are drudges, and we're all fools!"

"Don't you know it will never be any better for women until they have the right to vote?" Ben asked her. "What good would that do?" snapped Abigail. "Can't you see," Ben insisted patiently, "that women do half of the work of the world? And don't you know that if women were voters there would soon be law makers among them?"

A light dawned over Abigail, dazzling her like Saul on the road to Damascus. "The light permeated my very marrow bones," she remembered, "filling me with such hope, courage and determination as no obstacle could conquer and nothing but death could overcome." At 36, mother of six children, she had found her mission in life: equal suffrage.

On the flood tide of her new resolve, Abigail now proposed, though she had no experience whatever in journalism, to publish a weekly newspaper for women. For this purpose, early in 1871 the Duniways moved to Portland, then a town of about 8,000 inhabitants whose pioneer homes still nestled, in Abigail's words, "among fallen trees and blackened stumps."

The calling card of America's first woman mayor, Susanna Salter, bears her photograph. Placed on the ballot in Argonia, Kansas, by male "wets" as a trick to embarrass the local WCTU, she won easily.

For $40 a month, Mrs. Duniway rented the two upper bedrooms of a two-story frame house to use as her print shop. There she installed a foreman, at $25 a week, to produce the paper and teach her older sons the art of printing. Abigail herself wrote the editorial copy. With superb self-confidence, she put out the first issue of the *New Northwest* on May 5, 1871. It was to flourish for 16 years.

Her purpose, of course, was to achieve equal rights for her sex, but she knew better than to subject her readers to endless harangues. She would reach out and educate women by talking to them about their daily concerns. In a letters column, Abigail dispensed practical advice to anxious supplicants. "Nervous Sufferer" was firmly told, "You need *rest*. Get your decaying teeth extracted. Let Molly's face go dirty and John's knee peep out. These things will surely happen when you are dead and gone." She admonished a prospective bride: "You need not make a skirt with a train. Hope you are going to be a sensible helpmeet to your future husband and, if so, you must begin by dressing sensibly. A trailing dress is an emblem of degradation."

Abigail had a soft spot for fiction, and soon she was writing serial stories for publication in the paper: *Ellen Dowd, the Farmer's Wife* and *Judith Reid, the Plain Story of a Plain Woman*. They were homely narratives of domestic trials and triumphs, inspired by her own experiences and designed to illustrate her great theme: women were an exploited, subject race, "servants without wages."

In her editorial columns she dealt more directly with the matter of women's suffrage, lashing out caustically at her own sex when so moved. In Washington, D.C., she reported in one issue, a group of government wives had signed a statement denouncing votes for women on the ground that "Holy Scripture inculcates a different and for us a higher sphere, apart from public life." Not only that, they believed if they were given the right to vote, they might be expected to do things "unsuited to our physical organizations." Abigail's scorn was searing. "We toiling and tax-paying women, but reading and reasoning women," she wrote, "who stay at home while these parasites are flirting at the capital, do not care a single straw if they do not vote. A sensible exercise of their inherent right of franchise is doubtless 'unsuited to their physical organization.'"

Mrs. Duniway did not long have to rely solely on her own creative resources for fresh copy. Soon after the first issue of the *New Northwest* was published, the

A doughty trailblazer in fashion and in politics

Though few women won public office before the adoption of equal voting rights, many a frontier feminist ran to publicize her cause. One of the most persistent, Marietta Stow, took to the hustings four times, running for San Francisco school director in 1880, California governor in 1882 and then, as the first woman ever nominated, for Vice President of the United States in 1884 and 1888.

She endorsed protection of suffrage, widows' rights, racial equality, physical culture and family communes. She urged dress reform, which she emphasized by campaigning in odd attire *(below)* of her own design. Refusing to don "the long, uncouth drangling bag called a dress skirt," the formidable nominee chose "a skirt, 12 inches from the floor, stockings, leggings or trousers."

Vote totals for her first and third races were never recorded; for governor she polled less than 15 votes statewide, and for Vice President in 1888, she and Presidential running mate Belva Lockwood, a Washington, D.C., attorney, garnered only some 4,000 votes in seven states.

The initials of the Social Science Sisterhood, a California feminist group, adorn a ballot box *(above)* that Marietta Stow *(right)* used when she ran for governor. In those days voters dropped their ballots in the box of their selected candidate.

controversial Susan B. Anthony arrived in Portland to lecture on women's rights. Before Miss Anthony headed East again, her sojourn in the Northwest had stretched into months and taken her some 1,000 miles. During all that time, the *New Northwest* served as her mouthpiece and journal of record. Circulation boomed—and Abigail added yet another skill, public speaking, to her arsenal.

Calling at Susan B. Anthony's hotel the morning after Miss Anthony's arrival in August 1871, Abigail was worried. Like every other newspaper-reading American, she was well acquainted with the caricatures that portrayed the Eastern feminist as a quarrelsome, man-hating old maid and wild-eyed radical. To Abigail's profound relief, Susan B. Anthony in person was "a most womanly woman, gentle voiced, logical, full of business." Miss Anthony instantly decided that Abigail must accompany her, in the capacity of business manager, on a speaking tour of Oregon and Washington and must also deliver the introductory remarks at all of the meetings.

Though Abigail had never been at a loss for words, she had yet to utter any on a public stage. That was something respectable Victorian ladies simply did not do—unless they were willing to be pilloried like Susan B. Anthony. Thus she was genuinely nervous when she rose to introduce the famous visitor to their first audience—a "cold, curious and critical crowd" gathered in a Portland theater.

She need not have feared: her adroit little opening speech made a perfect prologue to Susan B. Anthony's "inspired" address, and together the two women converted several unbelievers on the spot. From that day on, Abigail was inundated with invitations to lecture, and she acquired such a taste for public speaking that she would spend a large part of the next 25 years barnstorming for her cause.

The peripatetic Mrs. Duniway became a familiar figure to stagecoach drivers and steamboat captains, scribbling copy for the *New Northwest* whenever she had a moment to spare, collecting an audience for her message wherever she could—in churches, theaters, at way stations, on the steamer docks. She found eager listeners and sympathetic friends; she also encountered spiteful hostility. The malicious gossiped that any woman traveling unchaperoned as she did was shameless: no doubt she drank and smoked, carried on in her hotel room, flouted her husband—an accusation that her family was quick to refute. Sometimes she had to face opposition as crude and explicit as the rotten eggs that rowdies threw at her in the southern Oregon mining town of Jacksonville—"Jacksonville arguments," she called them ever after.

Abigail was fearless in defense of her right to be heard. Once, at a temperance meeting in a church, the disapproving minister organized a choir of women to burst into song whenever Abigail got up to talk about suffrage. At the next meeting she sat silent, seemingly chastened. Then, during a momentary lull, she leaped to her feet and cried: "Let us pray!" While the minister glared, she addressed to the Almighty a forceful, 20-minute plea that every yoke might be lifted and the oppressed set free, and that bigotry and tyranny might disappear from the pulpit along with vice and tyranny from the saloon.

Meanwhile, Mrs. Duniway had become a lobbyist, and with encouraging success. Prompted by her efforts, the Oregon legislature in 1874 passed a Married Women's Property Act, stipulating that a businesswoman's assets could not be seized by her husband's creditors. And an 1878 measure gave women taxpayers the right to vote in school elections. But the great prize of equal suffrage remained elusive—because, Abigail believed, men resented the push for prohibition of alcohol that was being led by women.

Abigail herself had been an early supporter of temperance, but she firmly believed that outright prohibition would never work. More than that, she thought the issue would swamp the campaign for women's suffrage since men balked at giving votes to reformers who would dry up the saloons. And she was right. In 1884, when the Oregon legislature passed a constitutional amendment enfranchising women and the matter was laid before the voters in referendum, a contingent of WCTU speakers swarmed into the state to lobby for passage. Male misgivings stiffened into animosity, and the amendment was defeated.

The measure's most vehement supporter had done her eloquent utmost to push it through. On one occasion, making a speech in Salem's Marion Square to an attentive crowd, Abigail reminded her listeners with characteristic directness that the only Oregon citizens

A flag, with stars only for states granting
full suffrage, and a poster from Nebraska
are examples of the propaganda Western
women used in their campaign for votes.

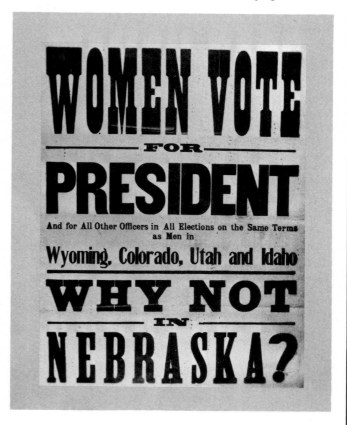

denied the right to vote were lunatics, idiots, crimi-
nals—and women. Fastening her sharp gaze on a small
boy who sat staring at her from one of the front benches, she said, "Don't you think your mother is as good as
any saloon bum?" The startled youngster blinked, and
stammered, "Sure I do."

His opinion nothwithstanding, the lad's mother
would have to wait more than a quarter of a century to
cast a ballot. For doughty Abigail Scott Duniway, the
1890s were discouraging years. She was gratified by
the extension of suffrage to the women of Colorado in
1893 and of Utah in 1896; her own efforts helped
materially to win suffrage for women in Idaho before
the end of the decade. Still the men of Oregon, perhaps
recalling the fall of Walter Moffett's Webfoot Saloon
to temperance crusaders in Portland in 1874, firmly
resisted the demands of their women for the vote.
Even in 1906, the year after Mrs. Duniway spoke in
honor of Sacajawea and the pioneer women of Oregon
at the Lewis and Clark Exposition in Portland, the

electorate turned thumbs down on suffrage for women.

The tide of prosuffrage sentiment kept rising, however, and in 1912, Oregon men finally gave their
women the vote. The state's governor, Oswald West,
called upon Abigail Scott Duniway, "that grand old
pioneer," to draft the Women's Emancipation Procla-
mation. Together they affixed their signatures to the
document. Governor West had been that little boy
who, 28 years earlier, had agreed with Abigail that his
mother was as good as any saloon bum.

And Abigail, victorious at last, stood recognized for
what she was: a trail-blazing spirit in the cause of
women's rights and the epitome of the indomitable
women of the Old West. If she had been a few years
ahead of her time when, facing the monument to Sacajawea in 1905, she had voiced her faith in the men of
Oregon, she could now truly hail "the liberty that is
dawning for the women of this western coast, where
man, chivalrous, patriotic, wise and free, is gladly wel-
coming his wife and mother to their proper sphere."

An enduring heritage of freedom for Western women

As the 19th Century neared its close, women in the West savored a self-reliance, freedom and sense of equality unknown to their Eastern sisters. Even the latecomers, those who had not actually crossed barren plains by wagon train, enjoyed the heritage of their bold female forerunners.

In some Western states they could vote and run for office, and Western land-grant colleges were leaders in opening their doors to women. In the West working women blazed new trails in careers once open only to men.

The women of the maturing frontier had other freedoms too. In a land still uncluttered by cities, they could relish the beauty of the outdoors and pursue the same sports men enjoyed—although often in unsuitable attire. Fashion was one tyranny that many second-generation Western women—perhaps recalling the sartorial privation of their pioneer mothers—happily accepted.

Colorado women fish for trout in the Rio Grande at Wagon Wheel Gap. Despite cumbersome clothing, they wield their rods expertly.

Young women from the University of Nebraska sprawl for a rest on a rocky slope of Pikes Peak with a male colleague during an excursion to Colorado. In spite of the rugged climb, they dressed in fine style.

Picnicking where earlier Western women may have feared hostile Indians or starvation, a dreamy-eyed Idaho mother relaxes with her family. Her spirited daughter, unable to sit still, was captured on film in an eternal blur of activity.

Skirts billowing high above their ankles, women dash down a rutted street in Sweet, Idaho, competing in a foot race at an Independence Day celebration in the early 1900s. Townsmen appear to be enjoying the spectacle.

PICTURE CREDITS

The sources for the illustrations in this book are shown below. Credits from left to right are separated by semicolons and from top to bottom by dashes.

Cover: From the Collection of Stanley Joselson, photograph courtesy of M. Knoedler and Co., Inc. 2: Courtesy Western History Collection, University of Colorado Libraries. 6, 7: Courtesy Wyoming State Museum. 8, 9: Courtesy Western History Collections, University of Oklahoma. 10, 11: Courtesy Patricia Stewart Baker Collection, Oregon Historical Society. 12, 13: Courtesy Montana Historical Society. 14, 15: Courtesy Peter E. Palmquist. 16: National Park Service, Homestead National Monument of America, courtesy of the Freeman family. 19: Courtesy Benjamin Gifford Collection, Oregon Historical Society. 20: John Zimmerman, courtesy Montana State Capitol Building. 22, 23: Library of Congress (3). 26, 27: Courtesy Kansas State Historical Society, Topeka. 28: John Zimmerman, courtesy Oregon Historical Society. 29: John Zimmerman, courtesy Lane County Pioneer Museum, Eugene, Oregon (2)—courtesy Museum of History and Technology, Division of Costumes and Furnishings, Smithsonian Institution. 32 through 35: John Zimmerman, courtesy Lane County Pioneer Museum, Eugene, Oregon. 37: Courtesy Nebraska State Historical Society. 38, 39: Courtesy California Historical Society/Los Angeles Title Insurance. 40, 41: Courtesy Wyoming State Museum. 42, 43: Courtesy Stuhr Museum of the Prairie Pioneer. 44, 45: Courtesy Seattle Historical Society, Museum of History and Industry. 46: John Zimmerman, courtesy Lane County Pioneer Museum, Eugene, Oregon. 49: Courtesy Moorhouse Collection, University of Oregon Library. 50: Courtesy California Historical Society, San Francisco (2). 53: Courtesy Peter E. Palmquist. 54, 55: Courtesy Panhandle-Plains Historical Museum—courtesy Denver Public Library, Western History Department—courtesy Kansas State Historical Society, Topeka; from the David R. Phillips Collection; courtesy Stuhr Museum of the Prairie Pioneer; courtesy Montana Historical Society—courtesy Doris Bacon Collection, Douglas County Museum. 57: Courtesy California Historical Society, San Francisco. 58, 59: Benschneider, courtesy Greeley Municipal Museums (9). 60: Benschneider, courtesy Colorado Historical Society. 61: Benschneider, courtesy Greeley Municipal Museums (4). 62, 63: Courtesy of the National Collection of Fine Arts, Smithsonian Institution. 64: Courtesy Arizona Historical Society, Tucson. 66, 67: Courtesy Library of Congress (4). 68: Courtesy National Archives and Records Service. 69: Courtesy Library of Congress. 70, 71: Courtesy Christian Barthelmess Collection, Miles City, Montana (2). 72, 73: Courtesy Library of Congress; from the Bob Lee Collection. 75: Courtesy State Historical Society of North Dakota. 76, 77: Benschneider, courtesy Kansas State Historical Society, Topeka—courtesy Collection of the Museum of American Folk Art, New York City, gift of Phyllis Haders; Tom Tracy, courtesy of the San Joaquin County Historical Museum, Lodi, California. 78, 79: From the Collection of John LaFont. 80, 81: Courtesy Denver Public Library, Western History Department. 82, 83: Courtesy Library of Congress; courtesy California Historical Society, Los Angeles. 84, 85: Courtesy Western History Collections, University of Oklahoma. 86, 87: John Zimmerman, from the Collection of Earl Henson. 88: Courtesy Library of Congress. 90: Courtesy Montana Historical Society. 91: Courtesy Nebraska State Historical Society. 93: Courtesy Roy Andrews Collection, University of Oregon Library. 94: Courtesy Nebraska State Historical Society. 95: Courtesy Idaho State Historical Society. 96, 97: Courtesy The Cherokee National Historical Society, Tahlequah, Oklahoma; Western History Collections, University of Oklahoma. 98: Courtesy Bernard and S. Dean Levy, Inc., New York. 99: Courtesy Western History Collections, University of Oklahoma. 100: Courtesy

Sisters of Providence Archives, Seattle, Washington (2). 103: Courtesy Montana Historical Society (2). 105: Courtesy Library of Congress. 107 through 109: Lady Cameron from the Collection of Janet Williams. 110: Thompson Historical Photo Collection. 111: Courtesy Oakland Public Library, California Room. 112: John Zimmerman, from the Collection of Dr. and Mrs. D. A. Fuesler. 113: Courtesy California Historical Society, San Francisco. 114, 115: Tom Tracy, courtesy Seattle Historical Society, Museum of History and Industry; Benschneider, courtesy Colorado Historical Society. 116: Tom Tracy, courtesy The Society of California Pioneers. 117: Duane Garrett, courtesy Idaho State Historical Society. 118, 119: From the Collection of Joe Erdelac, Cleveland, Ohio. 120, 121: Courtesy California Historical Society/Los Angeles Title Insurance. 122, 123: Courtesy Nevada Historical Society. 124, 125: Courtesy The Henry E. Huntington Library, San Marino; courtesy Ollie Beers Collection, Littleton Historical Museum, Littleton, Colorado. 126, 127: Courtesy Kansas State Historical Society, Topeka. 128: Courtesy Humboldt State University Library. 130: Courtesy California Historical Society, San Francisco. 131: Courtesy Colorado Historical Society. 132, 133: Courtesy Douglas County Museum. 134: Courtesy Colorado Historical Society. 135: Ted Sirlin, courtesy Wells Fargo Bank History Room. 136, 137: Courtesy California Historical Society/Los Angeles Title Insurance. 138, 139: Courtesy California Historical Society, San Francisco (2). 140: John Zimmerman, courtesy The Bird Cage Theatre, Tombstone, Arizona. 143: From the Mazzulla Collection, Amon Carter Museum, Fort Worth, Texas. 144 through 147: Benschneider, courtesy The Old Homestead Museum. 149: Courtesy Oregon Historical Society. 150: Courtesy California Historical Society, San Francisco. 151: Courtesy Cottage Grove Museum Collection, Lane County Pioneer Museum, Eugene, Oregon. 152: Courtesy Douglas County Museum. 154, 155: Courtesy The Bancroft Library. 156, 157: Courtesy Douglas County Museum. 158, 159: Courtesy Library of Congress. 160: Courtesy National Park Service, Yosemite National Park. 162: Courtesy Wells Fargo Bank History Room. 163: San Francisco Fire Department Museum. 165: Courtesy Library of Congress. 166: John Zimmerman, courtesy Mrs. William E. Cunningham. 167: Courtesy Arizona Historical Society, Tucson. 169: Courtesy Washington State Historical Society, Tacoma. 171: Courtesy Oklahoma Historical Society. 172: Courtesy Colorado Historical Society (3). 173: Courtesy Western History Collections, University of Oklahoma. 174, 175: Courtesy Arizona Historical Society, Tucson. 176, 177: Courtesy Della Phillips Museum, Tuscarora, Nevada (2). 179: Courtesy Kansas State Historical Society, Topeka (2). 181: Courtesy Library of Congress. 182, 183: Courtesy Denver Public Library, Western History Department (2). 187: Courtesy Elisabet Ney Museum, Austin, Texas. 188, 189: Courtesy Western History Collections, University of Oklahoma. 190, 191: Courtesy Solomon D. Butcher Collection, Nebraska State Historical Society. 192, 193: Courtesy Wyoming State Museum. 194, 195: Courtesy Moorhouse Collection, University of Oregon Library. 196, 197: Courtesy of the Anoka County Historical Society. 198 through 205: Kansas State Historical Society, Topeka. 206: Courtesy Denver Public Library, Western History Department. 207: Courtesy Nebraska State Historical Society; courtesy Nevada State Museum, Carson City. 210, 211: Courtesy Montana Historical Society. 213: Courtesy Miriam Matthews, Los Angeles, and the History Division, Los Angeles County Museum of Natural History (2). 214: Courtesy California State Library, Sacramento. 216: Courtesy Church Archives, Church of Jesus Christ of Latter-day Saints. 217: Courtesy Rell G. Francis Collection. 219: Courtesy David C. Duniway Collection, Salem, Oregon. 220: Courtesy Colorado Historical Society; courtesy Library of Congress (inset). 222: Courtesy Kansas State Historical Society, Topeka. 223: John Blaustein, courtesy The Oakland Museum History Department; G. D. Morse, courtesy The Oakland Museum History Department. 225: Henry Beville, courtesy Museum of History and Technology, Smithsonian Institution; courtesy Nebraska State Historical Society. 226, 227: Courtesy Colorado Historical Society. 228, 229: Courtesy Nebraska State Historical Society. 230 through 233: Courtesy Idaho State Historical Society.

ACKNOWLEDGMENTS

The index for this book was prepared by Gale Partoyan. The editors give special thanks to Dr. Gloria Ricci Lothrop, Professor of History, California State Polytechnic University, Pomona, who read and commented on the text. The editors also thank: George Abdill, Lavola Bakken, Douglas County Museum, Roseburg, Oregon; Dale Archibald, Elizabeth Buehler, Janice Worden, Oregon Historical Society, Portland; Fern A. Atkin, Alexandria, Virginia; Manon Atkins, Oklahoma Historical Society, Oklahoma City; Agnes Barchus, Portland, Oregon; Mrs. Casey Barthelmess, Miles City, Montana; Sister Rita Bergamini, Sisters of Providence Archives, Seattle, Washington; Neal Blair, Wyoming Game and Fish Department, Cheyenne; Glenna Booth, Denver, Colorado; Margaret Bret Harte, Lori Davisson, Arizona Historical Society, Tucson; Bonnie Brittain, Karl Fiechtmeir, M. K. Swingle, California Historical Society, Los Angeles; Janet Evelyn Brown, Citrus Heights, California; John Carter, Ann Reinert, Nebraska State Historical Society, Lincoln; Margaret Cavigga, Northridge, California; Florence Clark, Bernice Colson, Greeley Museum, Colorado; Jack Coffrin, Coffrin Gallery, Miles City, Montana; Frances Corsello, Denver, Colorado; Jim Davis, Idaho State Historical Society, Boise; Lynn Donovan, San Francisco, California; David Duniway, Salem, Oregon; Rell Francis, Springville, Utah; Bonnie Gardner, South Dakota State Historical Society, Pierre; M. A. Hagerstrand, Cherokee National Historical Society, Tahlequah, Oklahoma; Jack Haley, Don Ritz, Western History Collections, University of Oklahoma, Norman; Katherine Halverson, Wyoming State Museum, Cheyenne; Archibald Hanna, Beinecke Rare Book and Manuscript Library, Yale University, New Haven, Connecticut; Lodie Hern, The Old Homestead Museum, Cripple Creek, Colorado; Donald Jackson, Colorado Springs, Colorado; J. Roger Jobson, Deborah Ginberg, Society of California Pioneers, San Francisco; Alan Jutzi, Huntington Library, San Marino, California; Phil Kovinick, Los Angeles, California; John LaFont, Creede, Colorado; John Latimer, Terry, Montana; Bob Lee, Sturgis, South Dakota; Margaret Lester, Utah Historical Society, Salt Lake City; Dayton Lummis, Cripple Creek District Museum, Colorado; Marie MacDonald, Glendive, Montana; Glen Mason, Loretta Conger, Ed Nolan, Lane County Pioneer Museum, Eugene, Oregon; A. D. Mastrogiuseppe, Western History Department, Denver Public Library, Colorado; Miriam Matthews, Los Angeles, California; Steve Medley, Yosemite National Park, California; Florence Moffat, South Pasadena, California; Marjorie Morey, Amon Carter Museum of Western Art, Fort Worth, Texas; Joe Morrow, Judy Golden, Colorado Historical Society, Denver; Lori Morrow, Montana Historical Society, Helena; Mary Ellen Hennessey Nottage, Nancy Sherbert, Kansas State Historical Society, Topeka; Peter Palmquist, Arcata, California; Harold Peterson, Arlington, Virginia; Bill Slaughter, Church of Jesus Christ of Latter-day Saints, Salt Lake City, Utah; Cecilia Steinfeldt, Witte Memorial Museum, San Antonio, Texas; Nelson Wadsworth, Karen Weggeland, Brigham Young University, Provo, Utah; Mayor Fran White, City of Aberdeen, Washington; Virginia Perry Wilson, Napa, California; Janet Zich, Half Moon Bay, California.

BIBLIOGRAPHY

Alberts, Frances Jacobs, ed., *Sod House Memories.* Sod House Society Series, 1972.

Alderson, Nannie T., and Helena Huntington Smith, *A Bride Goes West.* Univ. of Nebraska Press, 1942.

Arrington, Leonard J., "The Economic Role of Pioneer Mormon Women," *The Western Humanities Review,* Spring 1955.

Bacon, Lenice Ingram, *American Patchwork Quilts.* William Morrow & Co., 1973.

Bancroft, Caroline, *Six Racy Madams of Colorado.* Johnson Publishing, 1971.

Barchus, Agnes, *Eliza R. Barchus, the Oregon Artist.* Binford & Mort, 1974.

Bass, Althea, *A Cherokee Daughter of Mount Holyoke.* The Prairie Press, 1937.

Beals, Carleton, *Cyclone Carry.* Chilton Co., 1962.

Beeton, Beverly, "Woman Suffrage in the American West, 1869-1896" (unpublished doctoral dissertation, Univ. of Utah, 1976).

Bentz, Donald N., "Frontier Angel," *The West,* July 1972.

Billington, Ray A., *America's Frontier Heritage.* Holt, Rinehart and Winston, 1966.

Blair, Kay Reynolds, *Ladies of the Lamplight.* B & B Printers, 1971.

Blegen, Theodore C., ed., *Land of Their Choice.* Univ. of Minnesota Press, 1955.

Bowers, Lola Garrett, and Kathleen Garrett, eds., *The Journal of Ellen Whitmore.* Northeastern State College, 1953.

Boynton, Searles R., *The Painter Lady, Grace Carpenter Hudson.* Interface California Corporation, 1978.

Brier, Warren, "Tilting Skirts & Hurdy-Gurdies: A Commentary on Gold Camp Women," *Montana, the Magazine of Western History,* Autumn 1969.

Brown, Dee, *The Gentle Tamers: Women of the Old Wild West.* Bantam Books, 1974.

Churchill, Caroline, *Active Footsteps.* Private printing, 1909.

Clappe, Louise, *The Shirley Letters.* Peregrine Smith, 1970.

Clark, Malcolm H., Jr., "The War on the Webfoot Saloon," *The War on the Webfoot Saloon & Other Tales of Feminine Adventures,* Oregon Historical Society, 1969.

Cleaveland, Agnes Morley, *No Life for a Lady.* Univ. of Nebraska Press, 1977.

Cooper, Gary, "Stage Coach Mary, Gun-Toting Montanan Delivered U.S. Mail," *Ebony Magazine,* October 1959.

Coues, Elliott, ed., *History of the Expedition Under the Command of Lewis and Clark,* Vol. II. Dover Publications, 1965.

Croly, Jennie June, *The History of the Women's Club Movement in America.* Henry G. Allen & Co., 1898.

The Daily Colonist, "Lone Woman Adventurer Never Carried Revolver," January 11, 1925, Victoria, B.C.

Davis, Ronald L., *A History of Opera in the American West.* Prentice-Hall, 1965.

"They Played for Gold," *Southwest Review,* Spring 1966.

The Denver Post, "Long Parade & Barbecue at Pueblo," July 4, 1905.

DeVoto, Bernard, ed., *The Journals of Lewis and Clark.* Houghton Mifflin Co., 1953.

Dick, Everett, *The Sod-House Frontier.* Johnsen Pub. Co., 1954.

Dielmann, Henry B., "Elisabet Ney, Sculptor," *The Southwestern Historical Quarterly,* Vol. LXV, No. 2, October 1961.

Drury, Clifford, *First White Women over the Rockies,* Vols. I, II & III. The Arthur H. Clark Co., 1963.

Duniway, Abigail Scott, *Path Breaking.* Schocken Books, 1971.

Earl, Phillip I., "Double Hanging Ends Odd Murder Case," *The Apple Tree,* August 24, 1975.

Faragher, Johnny, and Christine Stansell, "Women and their Families on the Overland Trail, 1842-1867," *Feminist Studies,* Vol. II, Nos. 2/3.

Feitz, Leland, *Myers Avenue: A Quick History of Cripple Creek's Red-Light District.* Little London Press, 1977.

Finley, Ruth E., *Old Patchwork Quilts and the Women Who Made Them.* Charles T. Branford Co., 1970.

Fischer, Christiane, ed., *Let Them Speak for Themselves.* Archon Books, 1977.

Flexner, Eleanor, *Century of Struggle.* Atheneum, 1972.

Fowler, William W., *Woman on the American Frontier.* Gale Research Co., 1974.

"Gilson Family Manuscript," unpublished manuscript, California Historical Society.

Gray, Dorothy, *Women of the West.* Les Femmes, 1976.

Guerin, Mrs. E. J., *Mountain Charley.* Univ. of Oklahoma Press, 1968.

Halliburton, R., Jr., unpublished manuscript, Cherokee National Historical Society.

Holdredge, Helen, *Firebelle Lillie.* Meredith Press, 1967.

Hopkins, Sarah Winnemucca, *Reproduction of Life Among the Paiutes: Their Wrongs and Claims.* Chalfont Press, 1969.

Horan, James D., *Desperate Women.* Bonanza Books, 1952.

Howard, Harold P., *Sacajawea.* Univ. of Oklahoma Press, 1971.

Jackson, Donald, ed., *Letters of the Lewis and Clark Expedition with Related Documents, 1783-1854.* Univ. of Illinois Press, 1962.

James, Edward T., Janet Wilson James and Paul S. Boyer, eds., *Notable American Women, 1607-1950,* Vols. I, II & III. Belknap Press, 1971.

Kelly, Fanny, *My Captivity among the Sioux Indians.* The Citadel Press, 1973.

Klose, Nelson, "Sericulture in the United States," *Agricultural History,* Vol. XXXVII, No. 4, October 1963.

Kovinick, Phil, *The Woman Artist in the American West, 1860-1960.* Northland Press, 1976.

Larson, T. A., "Women's Role in the American West," *Montana, the Magazine of Western History,* Vol. XXIV, No. 3, July 1974.

Loggins, Vernon, *Two Romantics and Their Ideal Life.* The Odyssey Press, 1946.

Love, Deanna Alice, "Dresses of the American Woman Pioneer in the Westward Movement from 1836 to 1889" (unpublished master's thesis, Univ. of Maryland, 1969).

Madison, Arnold, *Carry Nation.* Thomas Nelson, 1977.

Mazzulla, Fred and Jo, *Brass Checks and Red Lights.* Private printing, 1966.

Modjeska, Helena, *Memories and Impressions of Helena Modjeska.* The Macmillan Co., 1910.

Morgan, Ray, "Bender Mystery," *Kansas City Times,* March 5, 1953.

Munkres, Robert, "Wives, Mothers, Daughters: Women's Life on the Road West," *The Annals of Wyoming,* Vol. XLII, No. 2, October 1970.

Nation, Carry A., *The Use and Need of the Life of Carry A. Nation.* F. M. Steves and Sons, 1904.

The Oregon Journal, "Statue to Sacajawea, Heroic Indian Guide, Unveiled Amid Cheers of Multitude at Fair," July 6, 1905, Portland.

Owens-Adair, Dr. Bethenia, *Dr. Owens-Adair, Some of Her Life Experiences.* Mann and Beach, 1906.

Read, Georgia Willis, "Women and Children on the Oregon-California Trail in the Gold-Rush Years," *The Missouri Historical Review,* Vol. XXXIX, No. 1, October 1944.

Rhodehamel, Josephine DeWitt, and Francis Raymund Wood, *Ina Coolbrith.* Brigham Young Univ. Press, 1973.

Richey, Elinor, *Eminent Women of the West.* Howell-North Books, 1975.

Rinhart, Floyd and Marion, "Martha Maxwell's Peaceable Kingdom," *The American West,* Vol. XIII, No. 5, October 1976.

Rochlin, Harriet, "The Amazing Adventures of a Good Woman," *Journal of the West,* Vol. XII, No. 2, April 1973.

Roe, Frances, *Army Letters from an Officer's Wife, 1871-1888.* Appleton and Co., 1909.

Ross, Nancy Wilson, *Westward the Women.* Alfred A. Knopf, 1944.

Royce, Sarah, *A Frontier Lady.* Univ. of Nebraska Press, 1977.

Ruddy, Ella Giles, ed., *The Mother of Clubs: Caroline N. Seymour Severance.* Baumgardt Pub. Co., 1906.

Rutland, Mrs. J. W., *Sursum! Elisabet Ney in Texas.* Private printing, 1977.

Safford, Carleton L., and Robert Bishop, *America's Quilts and Coverlets.* E. P. Dutton & Co., 1972.

Schwartz, Mortimer D., Susan Brandt and Patience Milrod, "Clara Shortridge Foltz: Pioneer in the Law," *The Hastings Law Journal,* Vol. XXVII, No. 3, January 1976, © 1976 Hastings College of the Law.

Scrimsher, Lila Gravatt, ed., "The Diary of Anna Webber," *The Kansas Historical Quarterly,* Vol. XXXVIII, No. 3, Autumn 1972.

Segale, Sister Blandina, *At the End of the Santa Fe Trail.* Bruce Pub.

Co., 1948.

Settle, Mary L. and Raymond W., eds., *Overland Days to Montana in 1865: The Diary of Sarah Raymond and Journal of Dr. Waid Howard.* The Arthur H. Clark Co., 1971.

Shaw, Anna Howard, *The Story of a Pioneer.* Harper and Brothers, 1943.

Sibbald, John, "Camp Followers All," *The American West,* Vol. III, No. 2, Spring 1966.

Sinclair, Andrew, *The Better Half: The Emancipation of the American Women.* Harper & Row, 1965.

Smith, Helen Krebs, ed., *With Her Own Wings.* Beattie and Co., 1948.

Spooner, Ella Brown, *Tabitha Brown's Western Adventures.* Exposition Press, 1958.

Sprague, William Forrest, *Women and the West.* Arno Press, 1972.

Stallard, Patricia, "Glittering Misery: Lives of Army Dependents in the Trans-Mississippi West, 1865-1898" (unpublished doctoral dissertation, East Tennessee State Univ., 1972).

Stephens, Ira Kendrick, *The Hermit Philosopher of Liendo.* Southern Methodist Univ. Press, 1951.

Stewart, Elinor Pruitt Rupert, *Letters of a Woman Homesteader.* Univ. of Nebraska Press, 1961.

Taylor, Robert, *Vessel of Wrath.* New American Library, 1966.

Thane, James L., Jr., "Love from All to All: The Governor's Lady Writes Home to Ohio," *Montana, the Magazine of Western History,* Vol. XXIV, No. 3, Summer 1974.

Towle, Virginia, *Vigilante Women.* A. S. Barnes and Co., 1966.

Vogdes, Ada, "The Journal of Ada Vogdes, 1868-1871," *Montana, the Magazine of Western History,* Vol. XIII, No. 3, Summer 1963.

Vuolo, Brett Harvey, "Pioneer Diaries: The Untold Story of the West," *Ms. Magazine,* Vol. III, No. 11, May 1975.

Wellman, Paul I., *A Dynasty of Western Outlaws.* Bonanza Books, 1961.

Wilson, Carol Green, *A History of the Heritage, 1853-1970.* The Ladies Protection and Relief Society, 1970.

Wilson, Dorothy Clarke, *Bright Eyes.* McGraw-Hill Book Co., 1974.

TEXT CREDITS

Chapter I: Particularly useful sources for information and quotes in this chapter: Bernard DeVoto, *The Journals of Lewis and Clark,* Houghton Mifflin Company, 1953; Clifford Drury, *First White Women over the Rockies,* Vols. I, II, III, The Arthur H. Clark Company, 1963; Johnny Faragher and Christine Stansell, "Women and Their Families on the Overland Trail, 1842-1867," *Feminist Studies,* Vol. II, No. 2/3, 1975; Harold P. Howard, *Sacajawea,* University of Oklahoma Press, 1971; Robert Munkres, "Wives, Mothers, Daughters: Women's Life on the Road West," *The Annals of Wyoming,* Vol. 42, No. 2, October 1970; Georgia Willis Read, "Women and Children on the Oregon-California Trail in the Gold Rush Years," *Missouri Historical Review,* Vol. XXXIX, No. 1, October 1944; Sarah Royce, *A Frontier Lady,* University of Nebraska Press, 1977. Chapter II: Dee Brown, *The Gentle Tamers,* Bantam Books, Inc., 1974; Fanny Kelly, *My Captivity Among the Sioux Indians,* Citadel Press, 1973; Frances Roe, *Army Letters from an Officer's Wife, 1871-1888,* Appleton and Company, 1909; Nancy Wilson Ross, *Westward the Women,* Alfred A. Knopf, Inc., 1944; Patricia Stallard, "Glittering Misery: Lives of Army Dependents in the Trans-Mississippi West, 1865-1896" (unpublished doctoral dissertation, East Tennessee State University, 1972); Elinore Pruitt Rupert Stewart, *Letters of a Woman Homesteader,* University of Nebraska Press, 1961; James L. Thane Jr., "Love From All to All: The Governor's Lady Writes Home to Ohio," *Montana, the Magazine of Western History,* Vol. XXIV, No. 3, Summer 1974; Ada Vogdes, "The Journal of Ada Vogdes, 1868-1871," *Montana, the Magazine of Western History,* Vol. XIII, No. 3, Summer 1963; Brett Harvey Vuolo, "Pioneer Diaries: The Untold Story of the West," *Ms. Magazine,* Vol. III, No. 11, May 1975. Chapter III: Frances Jacobs Alberts, ed., *Sod House Memories,* Sod House Society Series, 1972; Jennie June Croly, *The History of the Women's Club Movement in America,* Henry G. Allen & Company, 1898; Josephine DeWitt Rhodehamel and Francis Raymund Wood, *Ina Coolbrith,* Brigham Young University Press, 1973; Lila Gravatt Scrimsher, ed., "The Diary of Anna Webber," *The Kansas Historical Quarterly,* Vol. XXXVIII, No. 3, Autumn 1972; Sister Blandina Segale, *At the End of the Santa Fe Trail,* The Bruce Publishing Company, 1948; Ella Brown Spooner, *Tabitha Brown's Western Adventures,* Exposition Press, Inc., 1958; Virginia Towle, *Vigilante Women,* A. S. Barnes and Company, Inc., 1966. Chapter IV: Caroline Bancroft, *Six Racy Madams of Colorado,* Johnson Publishing Company, 1971; Warren Brier, "Tilting Skirts and Hurdy-Gurdies: A Commentary on Gold Camp Women," *Montana, the Magazine of Western History,* Autumn 1969; Christiane Fischer, ed., *Let Them Speak for Themselves,* Archon Books, 1977; Helena Modjeska, *Memories and Impressions of Helena Modjeska,* The Macmillan Company, Inc., 1910; Dr. Bethenia Owens-Adair, *Dr. Owens-Adair, Some of Her Life Experiences,* Mann and Beach, 1906; Mortimer Schwartz, Susan Brandt and Patience Milrod, "Clara Shortridge Foltz: Pioneer in the Law," *The Hastings Law Journal,* Vol. XXVII, No. 3, January 1976, © 1976 Hastings College of the Law. Chapter V: *The Daily Colonist,* "Lone Woman Adventurer Never Carried Revolver," January 11, 1925, Victoria, B.C.; Henry Dielmann, "Elisabet Ney, Sculptor," *The Southwestern Historical Quarterly,* Vol. LXV, No. 2, October 1961; Mrs. E. J. Guerin, *Mountain Charley,* University of Oklahoma Press, 1968; Helen Holdredge, *Firebelle Lillie,* Meredith Press, 1967; Vernon Loggins, *Two Romantics and Their Ideal Life,* Odyssey Press, 1946; Floyd and Marion Rinhart, "Martha Maxwell's Peaceable Kingdom," *The American West,* Vol. XIII, No. 5, October 1976. Chapter VI: Caroline Churchill, *Active Footsteps,* private printing, 1909; Malcolm H. Clark Jr., "The War on the Webfoot Saloon," *The War on the Webfoot Saloon & Other Tales of Feminine Adventure,* Oregon Historical Society, 1969; Abigail Scott Duniway, *Path Breaking,* Schocken Books, Inc., 1971; Dorothy Gray, *Women of the West,* Les Femmes, 1976; Elinor Richey, *Eminent Women of the West,* Howell-North Books, 1975; Dorothy Clarke Wilson, *Bright Eyes,* McGraw-Hill Book Company, 1974.

Printed in U.S.A.